the religion is easy

the religion is easy

inspiration for those new to Islam

edited by

Adam Brown

Prophet Muhammad (peace be upon him) said:

"Truly, the religion is easy and no one burdens himself in religion but that it overwhelms him. Follow the right course, seek closeness to Allah, give glad tidings, and seek help for worship in the morning and evening *and a part of the night.*"

(recorded by Bukhari)

27 26 25 24 1 2 3 4

Published by Tughra Books
335 Clifton Ave.
Clifton, NJ, 07011, USA
www.tughrabooks.com

ISBN: 978-1-59784-967-8
Ebook: 978-1-59784-998-2

Library of Congress Cataloging-in-Publication Data

Names: Brown, Adam (Tughra Books), editor.
Title: The religion is easy! : inspiration for those new to Islam / edited by Adam Brown.
Description: Clifton, NJ, USA : Tughra Books, [2024] | Includes bibliographical references.
Identifiers: LCCN 2024022966 (print) | LCCN 2024022967 (ebook) | ISBN 9781597849678 | ISBN 9781597849982 (ebook)
Subjects: LCSH: Islam--History.
Classification: LCC BP161.3 .R4433 2024 (print) | LCC BP161.3 (ebook) | DDC 297--dc23/eng/20240706
LC record available at https://lccn.loc.gov/2024022966
LC ebook record available at https://lccn.loc.gov/2024022967

Contents

Introduction

Readership

As the subtitle of this book states, it is intended as inspiration for those new to Islam. This covers three groups of people:

Those who are totally new to Islam. That is, they know little or nothing about Islam. However, it is not a comprehensive introduction to the religion. Anyone wanting such an introduction should read one of the many books on the subject, e.g. Brandon Richey's *Islam from Scratch*[1]. Instead, this book covers major aspects of the religion, but not in a comprehensive way, for reasons outlined below.

Those who are interested in Islam and Muslims. Perhaps they have read articles about Islam in the media, and wondered whether what was written (usually by non-Muslims) corresponds to what Muslims actually believe. Perhaps they have heard about Islam and realize that it is a major world religion, and that they should therefore learn more about it, from first-hand sources.

Those who are converting to Islam, or have recently converted, and therefore only know the basics. The chapters in this book should fill in many of the gaps, and add to their knowledge of the background of the religion.

Conversion

While the final section of this book is entitled *Conversion*, this is not the primary aim of the book. The purpose of the book is to convey knowledge about Islam from an Islamic source. As recorded by Bukhari, Prophet Muhammad (pbuh – peace be upon him) said to his followers:

"Convey [my teachings] from me, even if it is one verse [of God's Quran]." The requirement for Muslims is thus to convey the message of Islam, not necessarily to convert anyone.

Conversion, especially by force, goes against the principle of free will, which underlies Islam and other world religions. In the Quran (chapter 2, verse 256), God states: "There shall be no compulsion in religion; the right way has become distinct from the wrong way. Whoever renounces evil and believes in God has grasped the most trustworthy handle, which does not break."

In this way, the person teaching about Islam receives rewards from God, regardless of whether the people they are speaking to eventually convert or not.

The religion is easy

The main title of this book is *The Religion Is Easy*, to emphasize the fact that Islam is not a difficult, exotic, austere religion, but one that is easy to understand, and easy to follow.

In fact, the title comes from a teaching (hadith) of the Prophet, recorded by Bukhari: "Truly, the religion is easy and no one burdens himself in religion but that it overwhelms him. Follow the right course, seek closeness to Allah, give glad tidings, and seek help for worship in the morning and evening and a part of the night." The Prophet advises people not to make Islam more difficult than it really is. He also lists some of the main components of faith: belief in God, doing good works, and the importance of prayer.

Writers

All articles are given here anonymously. The important element is the message, not the messenger.

Many people contributed material to *Rocket Science*, the now defunct newsletter of the Mount Albert Islamic Trust, Auckland, New Zealand[2], in addition to myself: Abdullah Drury, Abdur Rahaman, Azoora Ali, David Blocksidge, Farid Ahmed, Hady Osman, Idjaz Sheriff, M. C. A. Hasan, Dr Muhammed Ali, Nishaad Haniffa, Patrycja Sheed Ali, Dr Rishard Zuhair, Dr Sharif M. A. Fattah, Sheed Ali, Syed Akbar Kamal, Tazkiya Ali, and Wajahat Khan. This material formed the basis of the chapters of this book. Drafts of issues of the newsletter were proofread by David Blocksidge, and issues were loaded online by Sharif Nazre Hannan Saadi. May Allah reward all of them.

Thanks also go to David Blocksidge, Shaikh Rafat Najm, and Khairiah Abdul Rahman, among others, who commented on drafts of this book.

Language

As the majority of target readers of this book are people with little knowledge of Islam, Arabic has been avoided as much as possible. Quotations from the Quran come from the English translation of *The Clear Quran*[3]. (Similarly, English translations of the Bible come from the King James Version[4].) Explanatory notes not corresponding to the exact text of the Quran are given in square brackets [ ]. According to Arabic literary tradition, the Quran often uses *he* (*huwa*), but this often implies females too.

However, not all Arabic terms can be avoided. In places, the point being made is that Arabic terms have no simple English translation, and that they have often been mistranslated. Where Arabic terms are used, they are given in a simple transliteration into Roman alphabet. The purpose here is to identify the term and explain the concept, not to clarify small details of Arabic pronunciation.

To improve the readability of the text, scholarly references have been kept to a minimum. However, some are necessary, in order to show the origin of data, the source of word-for-word quotations, etc. Further details of all aspects of what is covered in this book can nowadays be found on the internet. Any reader wishing to find out more can always start at Wikipedia[5], but care should be taken, when finding out what Muslims believe, to access websites written by Muslims.

English books on Islam often use the following abbreviations:

swt: subhanahu wa taala "Glory to Him, the Exalted" (when mentioning God)

saw: salallahu alaihi wassalam "May the blessings and peace of Allah be upon him" (when mentioning Muhammad) as: alaihis salam "Peace be on him" (when mentioning other prophets)

ra: radi allahu anhu/ha/hum "May God be pleased with him/her/them" (when mentioning members of Muhammad's family, Companions, etc)

To improve the readability of the book – especially for non-Muslim readers – and in accordance with the house style of Tughra, these have been omitted. Muslim readers are encouraged to say them when reading.

Similarly, Muhammad is sometimes referred to in other books as *Muhammad, the Messenger, the Prophet,* etc. In accordance with Tughra style, these have all been expressed as *Prophet Muhammad (pbuh)* ("peace be upon him", the English version of *saw*) on first mention.

In line with English convention, epithets (nouns or adjectives) and pronouns referring to God are given with initial capitals, e.g. *the Pardoner, Almighty, Him.*

Finally, all dates are given according to the western Gregorian calendar. In non-Muslim circles, these are referred to as BC ("before Christ") and AD ("anno Domini", year of the Lord, i.e. Jesus). There are two problems with this. Firstly, nobody knows for sure when Jesus was born; many estimates put it at 4 BC. Secondly, while Christians may consider Jesus their lord, he is not a lord for Muslims and others. In Islam, he is a highly venerated prophet. For this reason, dates are referred to as BCE ("before Common Era") and CE (Common Era").

The Quran and hadiths

The two main sources for Islam are the Quran and the hadiths, and as in other Islamic books, they have been quoted extensively in this book.

The Quran, which Muslims believe is verbatim from God, was revealed to Muhammad piece by piece over 23 years, and constitutes 114 chapters. References to the Quran quote the chapter and verse. Thus "Have you considered him who denies the religion? It is he who mistreats the orphan, and does not encourage the feeding of the poor" (107:1-3) is verses 1 to 3 of chapter 107.

The hadiths are recorded teachings of Muhammad. There are six major hadith collections, compiled by Bukhari, Muslim, Abu Daud, At-Tirmithi, An-Nasai, and Ibn Majah. The collection is given after the hadith; some hadiths are contained in more than one collection, e.g. "Beware of suspicion for it is the most untruthful type of speech" (Bukhari, Muslim).

Adam Brown
Editor

1 Richey, B. (2021). *Islam from scratch*. Tughra Books.

2 https://mtalbertislamiccentre.org

3 Mustafa Khattab (2016). *The clear Quran with Arabic text: A thematic English translation of the message of the final revelation*. Furqaan Institute of Quranic Education. https://www.clearquran.com

4 *The King James Version* (1611). https://www.kingjamesbibleonline.org

5 https://www.wikipedia.org

1

The Pillars of Islam

The Pillars of Islam

Anyone reading an introductory book on Islam will quickly come across the so-called five pillars. These are the basic practices that all Muslims complete as part of being a Muslim. The description of the pillars in this section is not the rules pertaining to the pillars, the dos and don'ts, because they are presented in introductory books. Instead, the chapters describe background issues and explain the real purpose behind the pillars.

The first two chapters, on the pillars, explain that the purpose of them is to build moral character, and point out that they represent the minimum requirement for Muslims.

The concept of God (*Allah* in Arabic) is central to Islam. It is the first half of the declaration of faith (*shahadah*) that states that there is nothing worthy of worship except God (Allah), and Muhammad (pbuh) is His messenger. Declaring this makes someone a Muslim. The 99 names of Allah (*asma ul-husna*) are epithets that describe His nature. They may be nouns, such as *al-Razzaq* "the Provider" or adjectives like *al-Khabir* "the Aware". Three chapters elaborate on the nature of Allah.

Most people know that Muslims pray five times a day. The purpose of the prayers is to remind us of, and renew our faith in, Allah. In a recorded teaching (*hadith*), Muhammad said: "The first action for which a servant of Allah will be held accountable on the Day of Resurrection will be his prayers" (At-Tirmithi). It is therefore important that prayers are performed in textbook fashion, with full humility and concentration (*khushu*), so that they may be accepted by God. Two chapters give pointers on this.

Muslims fast for the lunar month of Ramadan. A chapter lays out the guidelines for fasting in Islam and other religions. Fasting means going without food and drink. However, its purpose is not to make you feel hungry and thirsty. The deeper meanings of Islamic fasting are examined.

Another central concept in Islam is charity. However, there are two types: compulsory charity (*zakah*) and voluntary charity (*sadaqah*). The differences between, and rationale behind, them are explained.

The final pillar is Hajj, the pilgrimage to Makkah. (*Makkah* is the more accurate transliteration of what in English is often spelled *Mecca*.) The financial, physical and mental demands on pilgrims are discussed, with tips to help you perform this once-in-a-lifetime experience with maximum ease and benefit.

The pillars have different timescales. The Hajj pilgrimage should be performed once in a lifetime. Fasting and paying *zakah* should be done once per year. *Salah* prayers are timetabled five times a day. Belief in Allah and His messenger Muhammad defines a Muslim, is a constant, and underlies all the other practices.

1 Morality and the pillars of Islam

Some Muslims believe that worship and morality are two different things. For example, they pray (*salah* in Arabic), but they lie. They give compulsory charity (*zakah*), but they cheat in other affairs. They fast (*sawm*), but they fall into performing forbidden (*haram*) actions. They perform the Hajj pilgrimage, but their hearts are sinful and impious. We cannot call them non-Muslims, because they have recited the declaration of faith (*shahadah*). However, we can distinguish good Muslims from not-so-good Muslims.

These are examples where Islam is practiced for appearance, or as a form of showing off to others. As a result, the substance and spirit of the beautiful religion of Islam is often missed.

Prophet Muhammad (pbuh) said: "I have only been sent to perfect good moral character" (Bukhari, Ahmad). That is, the purpose of the message that was revealed to him was to support the development of good character and instill morality into mankind. In this way, the world would be a better place for everyone to live and to receive the blessings of God (Allah). We may achieve this goal with knowledge and consciousness.

The five pillars of Islam are not mere acts without a purpose. Each one of them has a meaning and an application in our lives. These acts lead to contentment in our hearts and bring us closer to our Creator, God. They are far from being rituals and exercises that have no real meaning or application.

Shahadah

The *shahadah* is to declare that nothing is worthy of worship apart from God and that Muhammad was His final messenger. It is therefore known as the declaration of faith.

However, there are some believers who believe, but do nothing else. On the contrary, it is important that believers actualize their belief by carrying out moral actions, such as acts of charity, or helping the poor, widows and orphans.

In several verses of the Quran, God emphasizes that the two go hand-in-hand: belief and action. For instance, Surat al-Asr (#103) reads:

"By Time. The human being is in loss. Except those who believe, and do good works, and encourage truth, and recommend patience." By doing these good works, you show the strength of your belief.

Salah

Regarding the five daily prayers, God says in the Quran (29:45): "Recite [O Muhammad] what is revealed to you of the Scripture, and perform the prayer. The prayer prevents indecencies and evils. And the remembrance of God is greater. And God knows what you do." In other words, *salah* keeps us on the straight path. It gives us sanity, and keeps us away from doing wrong, not just to ourselves but also to other creations of our Almighty Lord.

Some hadiths are surprisingly short, but deeply meaningful. In a hadith recorded by Muslim, the Prophet said: "Prayer is a light." It is a light in that it gives us enlightenment and clarifies good from evil. It is said that the light is in your heart, and on your face, and will be in your grave, and on the Day of Judgement.

Prayer is a means of asking for forgiveness for any sins we may have committed. Abu Dharr, a Companion of the Prophet, reported:

> Once, the Prophet went out in winter. A lot of leaves were falling off the trees. When he held a branch of a tree, more leaves started to fall off. The Messenger of Allah said: "O Abu Dharr!" I said: "Yes, O Messenger of Allah!" The Prophet said: "If a Muslim performs prayers in order to please Allah, his sins will be shed like the leaves of this tree are shed." (Ahmad)

Zakah

Zakah is not only a duty for the rich and wealthy. It has a noble purpose, and aims to promote in all believers sympathy, kindness and benevolence. It also narrows the gap between the rich and the poor, and aims to bring about friendship and relationships of love for the needy, and the wayfarer.

Allah says in the Quran: "Receive [O Muhammad] contributions from their wealth, to purify them and sanctify them with it; and pray for them" (9:103). Thus Islam commands us to pay zakah. The literal meaning of the Arabic word zakah is "purification," in the sense that paying zakah purifies the remainder of your wealth. It also reduces inequalities between the rich and the poor, and raises the standards in the society.

Charity in general – not just zakah during Ramadan – is called *sadaqah* in Arabic, and involves all kinds of moral acts, not just monetary donations. Abu Dharr narrated that the Prophet said, concerning all kinds of charity:

> Your smiling in the face of your brother is charity. Commanding good and forbidding evil is charity. Your giving directions to a man lost in the land is charity for you. Your seeing for a man with bad sight is a charity for you. Your removal of a rock, a thorn or a bone from the road is charity for you. Your pouring what remains from your bucket into the bucket of your brother is charity for you (At-Tirmithi).

Fasting

Similarly, fasting (*sawm*) is also compulsory. It is not just about refraining from eating and drinking from dawn to sunset, but it is also about practicing self-restraint and keeping away from all haram things. It is also a form of worship. Fasting is encouraged for unmarried persons as it helps reduce carnal desires. It also cleans one's self, not only physically but also spiritually.

Ramadan is famous as a month of fasting. However, it is a period when Muslims should check other aspects of their everyday behavior. The Quran states the purpose of fasting as follows: "O you who believe! Fasting is prescribed for you, as it was prescribed for those before you, that you may become righteous [have *taqwa*]" (2:183). The purpose of fasting is thus not to feel hungry and thirsty. It is a prerequisite for trying to attain taqwa, a sense of God-consciousness.

Hajj

Often, people find it hard to relate Hajj to its purpose. They think that Hajj is merely a journey to Makkah and performing a set of actions. This attitude is incorrect. As God says in the Quran:

> The Hajj is during specific months. Whoever decides to perform the Hajj – there shall be no sexual relations, nor misconduct, nor quarrelling during the Hajj. And whatever good you do, God knows it. And take provisions, but the best provision is righteousness [*taqwa*]. And be mindful of Me, O people of understanding (2:197).

The compulsory element in Islam is that Muslims should perform Hajj once in their lifetime. Some Muslims perform it more than once. However, because of the physical activity and financial hardship involved, most Muslims perform it only once, thus fulfilling the requirement.

If you perform Hajj only once in your lifetime, it is important that you perform it in as perfect a manner as possible, so that it is accepted by God (known as *Hajj mabrur*). You therefore do not want to risk spoiling your Hajj by, for example, getting into arguments, or doing anything remotely haram. You should concentrate on doing what you have to do, and not worry about what others are doing. Because of the large crowds during Hajj, and occasional anti-social behavior, the word that people advise those going on Hajj to concentrate on is patience (*sabr*).

The purpose of Hajj is to join the community (*ummah*) of Muslims who have come from all corners of the world, to perform the compulsory acts obediently, and to grow closer to God and develop your morality.

The above is an outline of the relationship between the purpose and morality of the five pillars. They may differ in substance and form but, as stated at the beginning of the article, they all abide by the saying of the Prophet: "I have only been sent to perfect good moral character."

Surely man is at a loss if he is unable to purify himself and perfect his moral character. God says in the Quran:

> Whoever comes to his Lord guilty, for him is Hell, where he neither dies nor lives. But whoever comes to Him a believer, having worked righteousness – these will have the highest ranks. The Gardens of Perpetuity, beneath which rivers flow, dwelling therein forever. That is the reward for him who purifies himself (20:74-76).

2 More than the barest minimum

The following hadith of Prophet Muhammad (pbuh) was narrated by Talha bin Ubaidullah, one of the close followers of Muhammad, known as a Companion, and recorded by Bukhari.

> A man from Najd with unkempt hair came to Muhammad and we heard his loud voice but could not understand what he was saying, until he came near and then we came to know that he was asking about Islam.
>
> Muhammad said: "You have to offer prayers perfectly five times in a day and night [24 hours]." The man asked: "Is there any more [praying]?" Muhammad replied: "No, but if you want to offer the optional [*nawafil*] prayers [you can]."
>
> Muhammad further said to him: "You have to observe fasts during the month of Ramadan." The man asked: "Is there any more fasting?" Muhammad replied: "No, but if you want to observe the optional [*nawafil*] fasts [you can]."
>
> Then Muhammad further said to him: "You have to pay the obligatory charity [zakah]." The man asked: "Is there anything other than the zakah for me to pay?" Muhammad replied: "No, unless you want to give alms of your own."
>
> And then that man retreated saying: "By Allah (God)! I will neither do less nor more than this." Muhammad said: "If what he said is true, then he will be successful [i.e. he will be granted Paradise]."

It is an indication of the bounty of God that Paradise is given to Muslims who do the barest minimum requirement in respect of the five pillars of the faith. Notice that the Hajj pilgrimage is not explicitly mentioned in this hadith, although since the man was from Najd, which is the central region of Arabia, and was talking to Muhammad, presumably in Makkah or Madinah, he would have had little difficulty in fulfilling this obligation too.

Going the extra mile

Do we want to be Muslims who do the barest minimum? Or do we want to show the strength of our faith (*iman*) by doing more than this? It is always possible to do more in respect of our religious duties. Let us look at the pillars again, in reverse order.

1. Hajj

While the Hajj pilgrimage has to be performed once in your lifetime (provided you are physically and financially able), it is possible to do it more than once. Indeed, there are many people, such as clerics, *imams*, and other tour guides, who perform Hajj most years, leading groups of pilgrims. Many Middle Easterners, living close to Makkah, perform Hajj regularly.

It is also possible to go to Makkah at some other time of year. This minor pilgrimage is called *Umrah* and is optional, as opposed to the major Hajj pilgrimage, which is obligatory. The rites of Umrah are a small subset of the requirements for Hajj, and can be performed in a day. In contrast, the rites of Hajj require at least five days, and most pilgrims stay in Saudi Arabia for much longer than this minimum. Hajj must be performed in the first half of the Islamic lunar month of Thu al-Hijjah, while Umrah can be performed at any other time. And you avoid the Hajj crowds.

The minimum requirement for Hajj is focused in Makkah – especially Masjid al-Haram containing the Kabah – and takes in the areas of Arafat, Mina and Muzdalifah, on the outskirts of the city. However, there are three important mosques of Islam: Masjid al-Haram in Makkah; the Prophet's Mosque (*Masjid an-Nabawi*) in Madinah, containing the Prophet's grave; and the Dome of the Rock in Jerusalem (*Al-Quds*), from where Muhammad ascended in the Night Journey (*Al Isra' wa'l-Miraj*). While not compulsory parts of the Hajj pilgrimage, many pilgrims also visit those historical sites.

2. Zakah

While zakah has to be paid once per year, it is possible – indeed recommended – to give charity during the rest of the year, too. In a hadith, the Prophet said: "The believer's shade on the Day of Resurrection will be his charity" (At-Tirmithi).

Charity does not have to mean money, although it often is. It can be a gift in kind. In another hadith, the Prophet said: "Save yourself from Hellfire by giving even half a date-fruit in charity. If you cannot find this, then with a kind word" (Bukhari, Muslim). This emphasizes that the charity need not be substantial. In another hadith, he emphasized that charity should be regular. "The deeds most beloved in the eyes of God are those deeds carried out with continuity [regularity] although they may be small" (Muslim).

So again, you can easily give more than the obligatory zakat al-fitrah and zakat al-mal (see Chapter 10).

3. Fasting

Fasting the 30 days of Ramadan is compulsory. In some years, the lunar month of Ramadan is only 29 days.

As explained in chapter 9, fasting the 29 or 30 days of Ramadan is the minimum requirement. However, it was the practice of Prophet Muhammad (pbuh) to fast other days, too. Muslims are encouraged to perform voluntary fasts, according to his custom (the Sunnah), including:

- Monday and Thursday of each week
- The 13th, 14th and 15th of each lunar month, when the Moon is full
- Any six days in the month of Shawal (except Eid ul-Fitr)
- the first nine days of Thu al-Hijjah, especially the 9th, the Day of Standing at Arafat (this does not apply for pilgrims performing Hajj)
- as much as possible in the two months preceding Ramadan (Rajab and Shaban)
- the 9th and 10th days of Muharram, the first month of the lunar calendar

In a hadith, the Prophet said: "No slave fasts one day in the way of God without God putting his face seventy years' journey away from the Fire [of Hell] on account of that day" (Bukhari, Muslim). In other words, there are great rewards – both spiritual and health-wise – for fasting at other times.

4. Prayer

While the five daily prayers (*salah*) are compulsory (*fard*), there are many extra prayers that can be performed, both before and after the compulsory prayers and at other times.

There are two different activities that are captured by the English word *prayer*. The compulsory five daily prayers, involving particular numbers of cycles (*rakaah*), recitations and movements, are known in Arabic as *salah*. The different Arabic word *dua* literally means "calling," and covers any other prayer where you are asking God for something. To make this distinction, *dua* is sometimes translated into English as *supplication*.

The differences between salah and dua are given in the following table.

Salah	**Dua**
Compulsory.	Optional.
Five times per day, at particular times/periods.	At any time.
Must have ablution (*wudu*).	Need not have ablution (*wudu*).
Must be facing Makkah (*qiblah*).	Need not be facing Makkah (*qiblah*).
Must be in Arabic.	Can be in any language.
Four recitations are compulsory for the salah to be valid: * *Allahu akbar* * Surat al-Fatihah * Shahadah * Salam (saying *Assalamu alaikum* "peace be upon you" to your right, then left)	Any request can be made, using any words.
Particular stances and movements are compulsory.	May be made standing, sitting or lying. The hands are usually raised to about chin level.
	Optional duas may be inserted before or at certain points during the compulsory elements of salah. They are especially common after salah is completed.

So, you can do more than the minimum 17 cycles of prayer (rakaah) that are required per day in salah, and also add duas.

5. Shahadah

While the shahadah is the defining characteristic of a Muslim, and therefore something that is constant, this does not mean that we are constantly conscious of it. In other words, we can do more by reminding ourselves of God and his messenger.

This extra remembrance is known as *thikr*, and may take the form of repeating simple phrases. In a well-known hadith, Muhammad said: "There are two statements that are light for the tongue to remember, heavy in the scales, and are dear to the Merciful: *Subhan Allahi wa bihamdihi, Subhan Allah il-Athim* ("Glory be to God and His is the praise, (and) God, the Greatest is free from imperfection")" (Bukhari, Muslim).

There are a number of other thikrs we can recite which bring about different benefits.

Reading the Quran

Reciting any passage from the Quran, however long or short, brings rewards. You receive ten rewards for every letter you read – not every chapter (*surah*), or every verse (*ayah*), but every letter.

Subhan Allah* or *Subhan Allah wa bihamdihi

This means "Glory to God and Praise be to Him." The reward is that a tree is planted for you in Paradise (*Jannah*).

Alhamdu lillah

This means "All Praise is for God." On the Day of Reckoning, you receive a reward on your scales of bad deeds and good deeds.

Subhan Allah, wal hamdu lillah, wa la ilaha ill Allah, wa Allahu Akbar

This is a famous four-part thikr, meaning "Glory be to God, and all praise is for God, and there is no deity worthy of worship besides God, and God is Great." The combination of this thikr is beloved by God and sins fall off you.

La hawla wa la quwwata illa billah

Muslims who often say this thikr, meaning "There is no power or strength except by God", will enter Paradise (Jannah) through a special door.

Subhan Allah, Alhamdu lillah, and *Allahu Akbar*

It is recommended to say *Subhan Allah* "Glory be to God" 33 times, followed by *Alhamdu lillah* "Praise be to God" 33 times, and finally *Allahu Akbar* "God is Great" 34 times, giving a total of 100 repetitions. *Tasbih* beads allow you to keep count, and you can also do this on your fingers. Ideally, you should say this before you go to bed and after every salah.

Astaghfirullah

Meaning "I seek God's forgiveness", this thikr asks for protection from God's punishment.

Ayat al-Kursi

This is ayah 255 from Surat al-Baqarah (the second surah) of the Quran, and states:

> Allah! There is no god worthy of worship except Him, the Ever-Living, All-Sustaining. Neither drowsiness nor sleep overtakes Him. To Him belongs whatever is in the heavens and whatever is on the Earth. Who could possibly intercede with Him without His permission? He fully knows what is ahead of them and what is behind them, but no one can grasp any of His knowledge – except what He wills to reveal. His seat encompasses the heavens and the Earth, and the preservation of both does not tire Him. For He is the Highest, the Greatest.

This ayah praises God and celebrates His majesty. If you recite the ayah before you go to sleep, God sends a guardian angel to you and no devil (shaitan) will come to you until the morning. Those who read this ayah after salah will enter Paradise (Jannah).

La ilaha ill Allah

By reciting "There is nothing worthy of worship but God", the doors of Heaven are opened, and this thikr keeps the major sins away.

In short, all the pillars come with a minimum requirement and, according to the hadith at the beginning of this piece, even just that guarantees Paradise. Nevertheless, we can always do more with each one.

3 How does God refer to Himself?

This chapter looks at the way that God (Allah) refers to Himself in the Quran. Throughout, it should be remembered that Muslims believe that the Quran is the verbatim word of God, and therefore He is referring to Himself as the source.

We start with a bit of grammar. English examples are given, because this book is written in English, and its readers obviously understand English. However, the Quran is in Arabic, for the simple reason that it was revealed to Muhammad (pbuh), who spoke Arabic. As God says in the Quran (41:44): "Had We made it a Quran in a foreign language, they would have said: 'If only its verses were made clear.' [A] Non-Arabic [Quran] and an Arab [messenger]?" As we shall see, there are some important differences between English and Arabic.

A bit of grammar

In English grammar, pronouns are words that substitute for full nouns, often to avoid repetition of the noun or noun phrase: *I've bought a new car. It's a hybrid*, not *The new car is a hybrid*. There are three broad categories of pronouns. Throughout this discussion, a pronoun like *I* is taken to include its related forms *me, my, mine, myself.*

First-person pronouns refer to the speaker. In the singular, this is therefore *I*, and *we* in the plural (me and somebody else).

Second-person pronouns refer to the person being spoken to (the addressee or interlocutor, in academic terms). In English, there is only one word, *you*, regardless of whether it is singular or plural.

Third-person pronouns refer to anyone else, i.e. not the speaker and not the person being spoken to. In the singular, this is *he* for a male, *she* for a female, and *it* for anything else. In the plural, there is only one word, *they*, regardless of these distinctions.

In English, the picture is a bit more complicated than this:

Some speakers use non-standard *youse* (pronounced like the verb *use*) for the plural of *you*.

The singular 3rd person pronoun depends on the person's sex (*he/she*). But if the speaker does not know who it is, *they* can be used as a singular pronoun that is sex-neutral: *There's somebody at the door. What do they want?*

Cats and other pets may be *he/she*, or *it*. Cat-lovers will probably think of a cat as a member of the family, and personify it: *Felix loves sunbathing. He always sits by the window*. Others, however, will not personify it: *Beware of that cat. It scratched me.*

In a nutshell, that is the situation for standard English. Other languages may do things differently:

- Some languages distinguish *we* (me and you, i.e. 1st and 2nd person) from *we* (me and somebody else, not you, i.e. 1st and 3rd person).
- Some languages standardly distinguish singular and plural 2nd person (like *you/youse* in non-standard English).
- Some languages do not distinguish *he* and *she*, there only being one pronoun regardless of sex.
- Some languages distinguish *they* (male) from *they* (female).

In short, the three main determinants of pronouns are:

- $1^{st}/2^{nd}/3^{rd}$ person
- Singular/plural
- Male/female

However, the grammatical categories have some fuzziness in their use.

Capital letters in English

The commonest situation for capital letters in English, apart from the first letter of a sentence, is in names. These may be names of people (*John*), places (*Chicago*), countries (*Canada*), tradenames (*Pepsi Cola*), monuments (*Eiffel Tower*), vehicles (*Titanic*), etc. It is therefore appropriate that *Allah*, as a name, has an initial capital in English translations of the Quran.

Similarly, it is conventional in English to capitalize words that refer to God. Thus, pronouns like *He, Himself,* and *You* are capitalized when referring to God.

Epithets are words describing a quality or attribute. The 99 names of God (*asma ul-husna* in Arabic) are epithets. These may be adjectives such as *Loving* (*wadud*) or nouns such as *Creator* (*khaliq*). Note the initial capital *L* and *C* in English.

However, Arabic has no distinction between capital and lower-case letters, so this is a distinction that only occurs in translations.

Some oddities in English

There are two oddities that occur in English, and that will come in handy in explaining pronouns in the Quran.

1 The royal *we*

The first is the use of the plural *we* when the speaker is a singular person. This is academically known as pluralis majestatis (or majestic plural) or nosism.

It has ancient origins. In the Hebrew Old Testament of the Bible, God is referred to by the grammatically plural *Elohim*. The majestic plural started to be used in English by kings in the late 12th century CE, meaning "God and I", invoking the divine right of kings. It later came to be used by the monarch to imply that they were speaking on behalf of the country that they ruled ("my subjects and I"). The most famous example of this – although it may be apocryphal, i.e. not genuine – is the expression attributed to Queen Victoria: "We are not amused."

In 1989, Margaret Thatcher, British prime minister, said: "We have become a grandmother" on the birth of her first grandchild. This was met with disdain, as the royal *we* is meant to be used only by royals.

It was similarly used by former US president Donald Trump in tweets[1]: "But remember, WE are number one – President!"

In Indo-Aryan languages of the Indian subcontinent, the majestic plural is a common way for elder speakers and persons of higher social rank to refer to themselves.

So, the royal *we*, using a plural 1st person pronoun for a singular speaker, has for centuries been a common usage in different languages to show status.

2 Third person instead of first person

In certain circumstances, speakers use *he/she* or their name (a 3rd person device) when talking about themselves (known academically as illeism). For example[2], basketballer LeBron James justified his decision to leave the Cleveland Cavaliers and join the Miami Heat in 2010, by stating: "I wanted to do what was best for LeBron James and what LeBron James was going to do to make him happy" (rather than "what was best for me …").

In parent-to-child communication, a mother might say to a naughty child: "Mommy is angry with you. She's very angry with you."

So, that is the situation for English. Now we turn to the situation in the Arabic of the Quran.

Grammatical gender in the Quran

English has three 3rd person pronouns for different grammatical genders: masculine (*he*), feminine (*she*) and neuter (*it*). Arabic has only two: masculine (*huwa*) and feminine (*hiya*). This means that God can refer to Himself in the 3rd person as *huwa*. However, this is a grammatical phenomenon and does not imply that God is male or that He has a beard. Alternatively, He could use *hiya*. Similarly, this does not mean that God is female, for example, or that God can have babies. It is simply a grammatical constraint.

Grammatical number in the Quran

In the Quran, God sometimes refers to Himself, as one would expect, as *I* (*ana*), but also sometimes as *We* (*nahnu*). This may also be apparent from the grammatical form of the verb, which varies according to number.

The plural form (like the royal *we*) is used to express majesty, honor and high status. For example, the first verse (ayah) of Surat al-Kauthar (Surah 108) states: "We have given you plenty [al-Kauthar, a river in Paradise]." The use of *We* shows that God has the power to do this, and the authority to decide who goes to Jannah and sees al-Kauthar.

Does this mean that readers might misunderstand the fact that there is only one God? No. The following verse in Surat al-Kauthar continues: "So pray to your Lord and sacrifice." *Your Lord* is in the singular; it is not *your Lords*. This device, of following the majestic plural with a singular noun, is common in the Arabic Quran.

On the other hand, God uses the singular *I* when He shows unique love or anger. In Surat al-Baqarah (2:186), He shows His love and closeness by stating: "And when My servants ask you about Me, I am near; I answer the call of the caller when he calls on Me. So let them answer Me, and have faith in Me, that they may be rightly guided."

Grammatical person in the Quran

God refers to Himself in the Quran sometimes in the 1st person (*I, we*), and sometimes in the third person (*He, Allah*). And this may happen in quick succession.

For instance: "The command of God has come, so do not rush it. Glory be to Him; exalted above what they associate. He sends down the angels with the Spirit by His command, upon whom He wills of His servants: 'Give warning that there is no god but Me, and fear Me.'" (16:1-2). The 3rd person of the beginning of this passage (*Allah, Him*) stresses God's transcendence, while this changes to the 1st person singular of the ending (*Me*) in order to stress the unity of God, as well as to convey a warning.

God may refer to Himself in the 2nd person (*you*), but normally when He is instructing the addressee what to say. And again, this may alternate with other pronouns. This happens in some verses that all Muslims recite several times per day in their five prayers (Surat al-Fatihah, Surah 1): "Praise be to God, Lord of the Worlds. The Most Gracious, the Most Merciful. Master of the Day of Judgment. It is You we worship, and upon You we call for help" (1:2-5).

These changes of person (1st, 2nd, 3rd) may happen in rapid succession and lead to complex implications. For example: "No indeed! We created them from what they know. I swear by the Lord of the Easts and the Wests, that We are Able to replace them with better than they ..." (70:39-41). Neal Robinson[4] explains the various relationships here:

> The two pieces of first-person-plural discourse (the first and last parts) would be perfectly intelligible if read consecutively, ignoring the intervening material. God is the speaker, and His use of *We* is entirely appropriate in this context where He speaks of His power to create human beings. The temporary adoption of the first-person singular establishes the immediacy of the oath.[3]

Do these changes simply become very complex and confusing? Perhaps, to readers who are not native Arabic speakers. However, as Robinson explains, this is a feature of Arabic literature.

> Muslim specialists in Arabic rhetoric ... refer to this phenomenon as *iltifat* - literally "conversion", or "turning one's face to" - and define it as the change of speech from one mode to another, for the sake of freshness and variety for the listener, to renew his interest, and to keep his mind from boredom and frustration, through having the one mode continuously at his ear.

Az-Zarkashi, the 12th century CE scholar, wrote: "Moving from one style to another serves to make speech flow more smoothly, helps the listener to focus, renews his interest and avoids the boredom that may result from always adhering to one style."

Again, this may be hard for non-Arabic readers to appreciate, but it is an established traditional device in Arabic literature.

Muslims believe that the Quran is the word of God, and that God does things intentionally and does not make mistakes when He "speaks". The various forms of the pronouns and other epithets chosen by God to refer to Himself in the Quran are therefore not random.

1 RT (2019). 'The Royal WE': Trump derided for apparent megalomania in Twitter attack on comedians. *RT*, 13 March 2019. https://www.rt.com/usa/453719-royal-we-trump-jay-leno

2 Nordquist, R. (2018). Grammatical oddities that you probably never heard about in school. *ThoughtCo.* www.thoughtco.com/grammatical-oddities-not-taught-in-school-1692389

3 Robinson, N. (n.d.). Sudden changes in person and number: Neal Robinson on iltifāt. *Islamic Awareness.* https://www.islamic-awareness.org/quran/text/grammar/robinson

4 The All-Seeing

Why, when we go into a shop, do we not shoplift? Is it because the shop assistant may see us, and we may get caught? Or that the shop has security cameras, and we may be videorecorded shoplifting? Or that we know it is morally wrong to shoplift? Or that we understand that, by shoplifting, we are stealing from the shop owners, in what may be a family-run business and thus the source of income for the family?

This chapter examines how being observed may affect our behaviour.

A historical example of the consequences of (lack of) observation relates to the Argentina vs England quarter finals match of the 1986 FIFA World Cup, when Diego Maradona put the ball in the back of the England net for a 1-0 lead. However, England players immediately complained to the referee that Maradona had punched the ball into the net with his left hand, and slow-motion replays on television confirmed this.

The referee, Tunisian Ali Bin Nassar, did not have a clear view of the incident[3], and transferred the responsibility of awarding the goal (or not) to the linesman, Bulgarian Bogdan Dotchev. Neither the referee or linesman disallowed the goal. So, a worldwide TV audience of many millions could see the handball clearly, but the goal was awarded. Dotchev, who passed away in 2017, admitted that "the ghost of this match will probably haunt me to the grave. … Linesmen didn't have the powers they have now to disallow goals, call fouls for cards etc."[1]

In any case, it is doubtful that Maradona would have been able to head the ball into the net, as he was one of the shortest players on the pitch at only 1.65m, and the England goalkeeper, Peter Shilton, was 1.83m and could use his raised hands.

After the match, which Argentina won, Maradona brushed off allegations of cheating by stating it was "a little with the head of Maradona, and a little with the hand of God." This is untrue, as the ball did not touch Maradona's head in this incident, and it is doubtful that God would approve of such cheating.

Maradona would not have got away with such cheating today, because of VAR (video assistant referee). This is the technological system used in the top division of most countries, whereby all the cameras that are recording the play are linked to a control room, with a fourth official. Incidents can be replayed, and a decision made, such as whether a goal was legal, a player was offside, or a foul was worthy of a yellow/red card. If necessary, the referee can be called to view the incident in slow-motion replay on a monitor at the side of the pitch, and make the final decision.

In today's environment (and especially in a match as important as a World Cup quarter-final), VAR would have been consulted, the goal disallowed for handball, and Maradona probably shown a yellow card. In 1986 the goal was allowed and Argentina went on to win the World Cup.

Maradona himself later admitted that he punched the ball into the net. When asked what would have happened if VAR had existed in 1986, he replied, "I would have been arrested,"[2] for cheating in front of 80,000 in the stadium, and the worldwide TV audience.

Maradona, who passed away in 2020, will always be known as a cheat for this incident, despite his otherwise excellent football skills.

The All-Seeing in Islam

So, what has all this to do with Islam? The asma ul-husna are 99 names/epithets that describe the nature of God. Among them is *Al-Basir*, "the All-Seeing". Also among them are *As-Sami*, "the All-Hearing", and *Al-Alim*, "the All-Knowing, Omniscient". That is, Muslims believe that God is in control of this world and sees, hears and knows everything, whether it is open or hidden.

If we believe that God knows what you do and think, then we should be doing whatever pleases God, with good intention. That is, our behavior should be influenced by the fact that God is watching.

Muslims believe that God is watching, so we cannot claim that this is being done without our knowledge. He is watching us so that we may do the right thing and live a good life, following the permissible (halal) and avoiding the forbidden (haram). If, despite knowing this, we choose to do wrong, haram things, we know the consequences. On the Day of Judgement, our good and bad deeds will be shown to us. God willing, insha Allah, we will have done enough to be allowed to enter Paradise (Jannah), rather than Hell (Jahannam).

Ihsan

All the above is covered by the Arabic term *ihsan*. Its literal meaning is "beautification, perfection, excellence". It is often mentioned alongside Islam and iman. Islam is voluntary submission to God, expressed in practicing the five pillars of Islam. It is thus what we should do. Iman is belief in the six articles of faith. They therefore explain why we do the five pillars. The concept of ihsan is explained in the following well-known hadith related by Umar ibn al-Khattab, a Companion and the second leader of the Muslims (caliph) after the death of Muhammad (pbuh), and recorded by Muslim.

> While we were one day sitting with Muhammad, there appeared before us a man dressed in extremely white clothes and with very black hair. No traces of journeying were visible on him, and none of us knew him. He sat down close by the Prophet, rested his knee against his thighs, and said: "O Muhammad! Inform me about Islam."
>
> Muhammad said: "Islam is that you should testify that there is no deity except Allah and that Muhammad is His Messenger, that you should perform salah, pay the zakah, fast during Ramadan, and perform Hajj to the House, if you are able to do so."
>
> The man said: "You have spoken truly." We were astonished at his questioning him [Muhammad] and telling him that he was right, but he went on to say: "Inform me about iman."
>
> He [Muhammad] answered: "It is that you believe in Allah and His angels and His books and His messengers and in the Last Day, and in fate (*qadar*), both in its good and in its evil aspects." He said: "You have spoken truly."
>
> Then he [the man] said: "Inform me about ihsan." He [Muhammad] answered: "It is that you should serve Allah as though you could see Him, for though you cannot see Him yet [know that] He sees you." …
>
> Thereupon the man went off. I waited a while, and then he [Muhammad] said: "O Umar, do you know who that questioner was?" I

> replied: "Allah and His Messenger know better." He said: "That was Gabriel (Jibril). He came to teach you your religion."

This is often called the hadith of Gabriel. It succinctly explains the meaning of Islam and iman. It also gives a memorable and simple definition of ihsan: serving God and doing good, even though you do not see Him, because you believe that He is always watching you.

We thus have three levels of belief. Firstly, people may be Muslim (related to Islam) because they practice the five pillars. However, that is the bare minimum. Secondly, Muslims may additionally be *mumin* (having iman) because they believe in the articles of faith, some of which are unseen. Finally, Muslims may additionally be muhsin (related to ihsan), the highest level, that is, righteous people, doing good. Not all Muslims become mumin, and not all mumin become muhsin.

1 Asif Burhan (2022). Ali Bin Nasser says he would not have given Maradona 'Hand of God' ball. Forbes. https://www.forbes.com/sites/asifburhan/2022/11/02/ali-bin-nasser-says-he-would-not-have-given-maradona-hand-of-god-ball/?sh=af111cd157e8

2 As.com (2020). Maradona on Hand of God vs VAR: "I'd have been arrested." https://en.as.com/en/2018/06/01/soccer/1527856430_846226.html

5 The jugular vein

There is an often-quoted verse of the Quran: "We created the human being, and We know what his soul whispers to him. We are nearer to him than his jugular vein" (50:16). This does not mean that God (Allah) is physically closer to you than your jugular vein. Instead, it refers to His knowledge of you and His power over you.

Some commentators say that it could refer to the angels Raqib and Atid appointed to you, who sit on your right and left shoulders, noting everything you say and do. The angel on your right shoulder records all your good deeds, while the one on your left records bad deeds. The above passage from the Quran continues: "As the two recording angels – one sitting to the right, and the other to the left – note everything, not a word does a person utter without having a vigilant observer ready to write it down" (50:17-18).

A hadith states:

> The [scribe] on the left hand raises his pen [i.e. delays writing] for six hours before he records the sinful deed of a Muslim. If [the Muslim] regrets it and seeks God's forgiveness, the deed is not recorded; otherwise it is recorded as one deed (At-Tabarani).

This shows the importance and power of repentance (*taubah*) in Islam.

Position and medical purpose

We have all heard of the jugular vein. But are we familiar with where it is, and why it is important?[1] The jugular vein, like most veins in the circulatory system, carries deoxygenated blood from body tissues back to the heart. The jugular is a vein that carries a relatively large volume of blood from the tissues of the head and brain back towards the heart.

There are actually four jugular veins, two on each side of the neck. The internal jugular veins are much larger than the external ones, and therefore better known. The external jugular veins collect most of the deoxygenated blood from the outside of the skull and the deeper parts of the face, while the internal jugular veins collect blood from the brain.

The word *jugular* is related to two Latin words: *jugulum*, meaning 'collarbone' or 'throat,' and *jugum*, meaning 'yoke.'

If an internal jugular vein is opened or punctured, death can result very quickly from loss of blood, because of the quantity of blood carried by these veins. Hence the English expression "go for the jugular", meaning to attack a very vulnerable or vital part. In a more metaphorical sense, it means to attack fiercely in order to have no doubt about winning, or to criticize someone very cruelly by talking about what you know will hurt them most.

The jugular vein is sometimes erroneously portrayed as being the entire front of the throat or neck. In reality, while the jugular is a vulnerable spot, it still takes some degree of precision to injure it. Accidental injury is still possible, of course, as was the case with Archduke Franz Ferdinand of Austria. He was killed in Sarajevo in 1914 in a famous assassination leading to the start of World War I. Earlier in the day, his car was attacked by a Bosnian Serb with a grenade that missed the Archduke's car but injured people in the next car in the procession. A bit later, the Archduke insisted on visiting the injured in hospital. However, nobody had informed the drivers of the change of itinerary. As the cars tried to turn round, the procession came to a halt, and another Bosnian Serb seized the opportunity to attack. A bullet hit the Archduke in the jugular vein, causing his rapid death from blood loss.

In some cases, the position of the jugular veins can be visible from the outside. If a jugular vein is particularly prominent when a person is in a sitting position, it can be a sign of congestive heart failure. The height or prominence of these veins can be a good indicator, in this case, of how well the heart is keeping up with the demands placed upon it, or if it is failing to do so.

The metaphor

The Quranic verse contains a wonderful metaphor. So, how is God's knowledge of, power over, and care for, you similar to your jugular vein?

Both are vital to your existence. Like other veins, the jugular has periodically spaced valves that only allow the blood to flow in one direction. Without these valves, the circulatory system could become inefficient or even be damaged due to the backflow of blood in the system.

An abnormal jugular is symptomatic of a malfunctioning heart. In order to avoid the darker nature of our baser instincts (*nafs* in Arabic), we need a properly functioning relationship with our Creator.

Just as the internal jugular veins convey the blood that comes from your brain, so God knows the thoughts that come from your brain. Whether we hide our emotions by disguising the expressions on our face or not, the external jugular veins transport blood that has flowed through the muscles required for such non-verbal communication. Similarly, God knows our emotions, whether we show them or not.

1 Hill, A. (2023). What is the jugular vein? The Health Board. https://www.thehealthboard.com/what-is-the-jugular-vein.htm

6 Mistakes in salah

The five obligatory daily prayers (*salah*) are among the pillars of Islam. They are also the most regularly performed action among the pillars. While a Muslim may be financially or physically incapable of performing Hajj, and thus not perform it in their lifetime, there is no such obstacle to performing *salah*:

> The first action for which a servant of Allah will be held accountable on the Day of Resurrection will be his prayers. If they are in order, he will have prospered and succeeded. If they are lacking, he will have failed and lost. (At-Tirmithi and others)

Therefore, it is important to perform this duty without any hesitation. At the same time, one must make every effort to perform it in the perfect way it is supposed to be performed. This chapter explains some common mistakes committed during salah which can nullify our salah or, if not, they do not completely invalidate it, they take its essence away.

Leaving salah altogether

Needless to say, not performing obligatory prayers is a mistake. It is such a central defining aspect of being a Muslim, and is a commitment taken when converting to Islam.

In the Quran (20:14), God says: “I am God. There is no God but I. So serve Me, and practice the prayer for My remembrance.”

The same message is contained in various hadiths. “A Bedouin with unkempt hair came to Allah’s Messenger and said: ‘O Allah’s Messenger! Inform me what Allah has made compulsory for me as regards the prayers.’ He replied: ‘You have to offer perfectly the five compulsory prayers [salah] in a day and night [24 hours], unless you want to pray Nawafil [optional extra prayers].’ (Bukhari)

Delaying salah intentionally

This is a common mistake in prayer made by many. Busy in our worldly affairs, we often delay salah from its allotted time. We think that praying is the last thing to do and we must attend to other matters first.

Many workers delay Thuhr and Asr prayer until nighttime. In the Quran (2:238), God speaks strictly on guarding our salah: “Guard strictly the [five obligatory] prayers, especially the middle prayer [Asr].” Here, “to safeguard the salah” means to perform it at its prescribed time and to be steadfast upon it.

Anas ibn Malik, a Companion, said: “I heard the Messenger of God saying: ‘This is the prayer of the hypocrites: He sits watching the Sun decline until it is between the two horns of Satan, then he quickly pecks the ground four times while he only remembers Allah for a few moments’” (Muslim). Thus, someone may perform four-rakaah Asr prayer just before sunset, at the end of its period, and then wait a short while for sunset, the start of the Maghrib period. They thus perform two prayers at one time, rather than at two separate times.

Therefore, one must make every effort to complete each prayer at its right time and, if we do not, there is very little doubt that we also label ourselves hypocrites, as indicated by the above hadiths.

It is also recommended to perform salah early in its period, that is, not long after the call to prayer (*athan*). We should not, for example, delay Thuhr prayer until just before the athan for Asr prayer, so that, by the time we finish Thuhr, it is already Asr. While this is performing each prayer within its period, it is not according to the spirit of salah. The important part of salah is that it is spaced out during the day, and we remember God at least five times per day. Delaying prayer until just before the next prayer destroys the regularity of this thikr. In a Bukhari hadith, Muhammad was asked: “Which deed is the dearest to Allah?” and he replied: “To offer the prayers at their early stated fixed times.”

Abandoning congregational prayer in the mosque

The commandment has been given to able men to perform Friday midday prayer in congregation in the mosque. Congregational prayer is a duty, except for those who have a valid excuse according to the Shariah. Muhammad said: “Whoever hears the call and thereafter does not answer it [i.e. does not attend the congregational salah], there is no salah for him, except for a valid excuse” (Ibn Majah and others). God also says: “And bow down with those who bow down” (Quran 2:43). In a hadith recorded by Muslim, the Prophet said: “If anyone performs ablution (wudu) properly, then comes to the Friday prayer, listens to the sermon (khutbah) attentively and keeps silent, his (minor) sins between that Friday and the following Friday will be forgiven, with the addition of three more days."

Performing the salah hastily

Salah should be performed slowly and calmly. Bending (*ruku*) or prostrating (*sujud*) must be performed unhurriedly. In order to complete the ruku, you must stay in ruku posture long enough until your limbs come to a complete standstill and you have enough time to recite *Subhana rabbi al-athim* ("Glory be to my Lord the Most Great") at least three times. In the same manner, for sujud, the person should say *Subhana rabbi al-ala* ("Glory be to my Lord Most High") three times slowly.

The following hadith commands us to complete the ruku and sujud in a proper manner. "Prophet Muhammad said: 'The worst thief is the one who steals from his own prayer.' People asked: 'O Prophet! How could one steal from his own prayer?' He said: 'By not completing its ruku and sujud'" (At-Tabarani). Muhammad also said: "He who does not complete his ruku and sujud, his prayer is void" (Abu Daud).

Lack of proper humility in salah and excessive movement

The place of humility, reverence and concentration (*khushu*) is in the heart and it is evident in the tranquility of the limbs. God has indeed praised His slave by His statement: "Those who are humble in their prayers" (Quran 23:2). He has also praised the prophets by his statement: "Verily they used to hasten on to do good deeds and they used to call upon Us with hope and fear, and used to humble themselves before Us" (Quran 21:90).

The limbs of the slave in prayer should be still and his heart should be solemn until he may be rewarded for his salah. In a hadith, Muhammad said: "Verily a man leaves after completing his prayer and nothing has been written for him except a tenth of his salah, a ninth, an eighth, a seventh, a sixth, a fifth, a fourth, a third, or half of it" (Abu Daud, An-Nasai, and others). The reason for the shortcoming in its reward is the lack of khushu in the heart of the one who prays, or in the limbs.

Gazing right, left or upwards during salah

While performing salah, one should concentrate on looking ahead and down to the point where the head is placed during sujud, rather than looking left, right or upwards, because this may destroy concentration.

Muhammad said: "Let those who raise their gaze up during prayer stop doing so, or else their sights would not return to them [i.e. they will lose their eyesight]" (Muslim).

Walking in front of a praying person

It is a sin upon the person who passes in front of someone who is praying. If there is no visible line before one who is praying, then a passer-by should pass beyond the point of prostration. Muhammad said: "If the one who passes in front of the praying person knew how serious a sin it was for him to do so, it would have been better for him to wait for forty than walk in front of him" (Bukhari, Muslim). "Forty" may refer to forty days, months or years, and God knows best.

Eating food of bad smell before performing prayers

Foods that have a bad smell, like garlic or onion, should not be eaten before the salah because the bad smell may irritate the angels and the worshipers. Muhammad said: "He who eats from the smelly plant [garlic or onion], let him not come near our mosque; the angels are bothered by that which bothers men" (Muslim). He also encouraged oral hygiene by brushing the teeth: "If it were not for fear that I would place hardship on my community, or on people, I would have ordered them to use the tooth stick at every prayer" (Bukhari).

Raising the voice in recitation to the point of distracting those around you

It is recommended (*mustahab*) that one hears oneself, but not to the point that it interrupts anyone who is reciting the Quran or making salah.

> Prophet Muhammad prayed Thuhr and there was a man behind him reciting *Sabbihisma rabbi al-ala* [Quran 87:1]. So when

> Muhammad finished, he asked: "Who among you was reciting or who was the reciter?" The man said: "Me." So Muhammad said: "I thought that some of you were disputing with me in it" (Bukhari, Muslim).

Scholars agree that the meaning of his words is a disapproval of the act of loud recitation in prayer.

Not making the rows straight

When praying next to someone, as in congregational prayers, you should be close. Muhammad stated:

> Straighten the rows! Align your shoulders to each other's, fill the gaps and be soft to your brother's hand, do not leave an empty space for Shaitan within the rows. Whoever joins the rows, Allah will join him. Whoever breaks the rows, Allah will break him (Abu Daud).

The rows in congregational prayer should be as straight as possible. This is often simple, as the carpet in a mosque, or the prayer mats that have been laid out, should be straight and facing Makkah (the *qiblah*). Nobody should be slightly forward of or behind the others. The imam, who leads the prayer, should stand alone in a central position in front of the first row. The followers should form rows behind the imam, completing any row before starting a new one behind.

Moving before the imam

One should not race with the prayer leader (imam), that is, try to move before the imam or with the imam. The imam is the prayer leader; he should lead and the followers should follow. Muhammad stated: "Surely the imam is there to be followed" (Muslim).

Closing the eyes for no reason

This is an objectionable (*makruh*) act as mentioned by Ibn Al-Qayyim, a 13th-14th century CE scholar: "Closing the eyes was not from the guidance of Prophet Muhammad." He also said:

However, the scholars of fiqh have differed on its detestability. Imam Ahmed and others deemed it detestable, and they said that it was of the habits of the Jews. However, a group of other scholars have ruled it allowable without any detestability and they said that it may indeed be a closer means of achieving khushu which is the spirit of the salah, its heart and its aim. Most correct is that, if keeping the eyes open has no detrimental effect upon khushu, then it is preferable to do it. If decorations, adornments or the like are around the worshipper or between him and the qiblah to the point of distraction, then there is no objection to closing the eyes. Indeed, the statement that to do so is desirable (*mustahab*) in this case is closer to the spirit of the law and its aims than the statement that it is objectionable. And Allah knows best.[1]

Recitation of the Quran in ruku or during sujud

This is prohibited, based on a narration from Ibn Abbas that Muhammad said: "I have been prevented from reciting the Quran while bowing or in prostration" (Muslim). Ali, the cousin and son-in-law of Muhammad, narrates: "Prophet Muhammad prevented me from reciting the Quran while bowing or prostrating" (Muslim and others).

When praying, we should always bear in mind who we are praying to, namely God. The various positions and movements, and things that need to be said, are standard, with very few minor variations between different schools of thought (mathhabs). We should therefore try our utmost to perform prayers in this standard way each time we pray, with full humility and concentration; this is the topic of the next chapter.

1 Ibn Al-Qayyim (1350). Zaad al-maad ("Provision of the hereafter"). https://www.allahsword.com/ebooks/Knowledge/Complete%20-%20Zaad%20al%20Maad.pdf

7 Concentration in salah

Sometimes our prayers (salah) seem to go like this: "Bismillah ir-rahman ir-rahim. Alhamdu lillah … (thoughts) this is a nice prayer mat. I wonder where that mosque is. It's not Makkah. Maybe it's the Prophet's Mosque. No it can't be – the color of the dome is wrong. Perhaps it's just a generic picture of a mosque … waladdallin." Before you know it, you have said your prayers on automatic pilot. Although you may have said the right Arabic words, you have said them with very little concentration or understanding. It seems preferable to say one rakaah with total concentration, than 20 without.

The fact that Muslim prayers are composed of differing numbers of the same cycles of prayer (*rakaah*) may lead worshippers to absent-mindedness and autopilot.

What follows are some ideas for breaking the routine of saying prayers, thus allowing us to maintain concentration in our regular prayers. The suggestions are illustrated by Surat al-Fatihah (#1), although the principles can be applied to any recitation.

Use a plain prayer mat or carpet

Many prayer mats are decorated with pictures of mosques or the Kabah. Similarly, the carpets in many mosques have designs on them in the form of flowers and the like. As the first paragraph illustrated, this may lead some worshipers to lose concentration. Especially with heavily decorated carpets, worshipers may start day-dreaming and seeing faces, birds, and other animals in the pattern.

There are two simple solutions. Firstly, use a plain mat or carpet. Secondly, as discussed in the previous chapter, it is permissible under such circumstances to pray with the eyes closed, in order to avoid these distractions.

Slow down

We always seem to say Surat al-Fatihah at breakneck speed. This does not help us to contemplate its meaning. The first suggestion is thus to deliberately recite the surah at half speed: "B.i.s.m.i.l.l.a.h i.r.r.a.h.m.a.n i.r.r.a.h.i.m a.l.h.a.m.d.u l.i.l.l.a.h i.r.r.a.b.b i.l.a.l.a.m.i.n." It is not surprising that we cannot ponder the meaning of the verse if we say it so fast that it is over before we know it. Slowing down allows us to reflect on the meaning, especially if Arabic is not our native language. In the Quran, God says: "… and chant the Quran rhythmically" (73:4).

Pause at the end of each verse

Several hadiths report that Prophet Muhammad (pbuh) interrupted his recitation, pausing at the end of every verse. So, he would say: "Al-hamdu lillah ir-rabb il-alamin", and pause; "ar-rahman ir-rahim", and pause; "Maliki yawm id-deen" … and so on (At-Tirmithi, Abu Daud, Ahmad).

This has two advantages. Firstly, it will help us to avoid speeding up. Secondly, it allows us to reflect on the meaning of the ayah we have just recited, and to enjoy God's reply to our prayer.

In a Bukhari hadith, Muhammad explained that God answers prayers, including Surat al-Fatihah:

> When the servant says: "Praise be to God, Lord of the Worlds", Allah the Most High says: "My servant has praised Me." And when he says: "The Most Gracious, the Most Merciful", Allah the Most High says: "My servant has lauded Me." And when he says: "Master of the Day of Judgement", He remarks: "My servant has glorified Me" and sometimes He would say: "My servant entrusted [his affairs] to Me." And when he says: "It is You we worship, and upon You we call for help", He says: "This is between Me and My servant, and My servant will receive what he asks for." Then, when he says: "Guide us to the straight path, the path of those You have blessed, not of those against whom there is anger, nor of those who are misguided", He says: "This is for My servant, and My servant will receive what he asks for."

Translate it (in your head) as you go along

Most of us are not native Arabic speakers. Arabic is thus less meaningful to us than our native language. Another way to reflect on the meaning of the Quran, rather than to recite it as less meaningful sounds, is to say each line in Arabic, then translate it in your head into the language you are most familiar with.

(Recite) Bismillah ir-rahman ir-rahim

(Think, in your head) "In the name of God, most Gracious, most Merciful"

(Recite) Alhamdu lillah ir-rabb il-alamin

(Think, in your head) "Praise be to God, the sustainer of the worlds"

This method also has the advantage of slowing down our recitation, as we will pause after each ayah, to translate it.

Concentrate on correct Arabic pronunciation

If you recite the Quran slowly, you are more likely to concentrate on correct Arabic pronunciation. For instance, some people recite "Sirat al-lazina an amta alaihim". Zat is not ze right way to say zis sound! They probably do this because the *th* sound as in *this, that and the other* does not occur in their native language. Nevertheless, it is a regular Arabic consonant sound, and should be pronounced correctly. Umm Salamah, a wife of the Prophet, was once asked by someone how Muhammad used to recite the Quran. She said: "In a way that all vowel sounds were clear and the pronunciation of each letter was distinct."[1]

If that is how Muhammad recited it, then that is how we should recite it, to the best of our ability. Many Muslims are not native speakers of Arabic, and many are converts, and so learning to pronounce the Quran correctly is a struggle. A beautiful hadith describes the rewards for that struggle: Aishah, his wife, relates that Muhammad said:

> Verily the one who recites the Quran beautifully, smoothly, and precisely, he will be in the company of the noble and obedient angels. And as for the one who recites with difficulty, stammering or stumbling through its verses, then he will have twice that reward (Bukhari, Muslim).

Think of gestures

As anyone who has taught oral presentation skills will tell you, an important channel that should be exploited in order to get the message across, and make it more meaningful and memorable, is to use gestures and other nonverbal features. While these cannot actually be used while reciting prayers, you can make them mentally in your head. While some examples are given below, you should think of whatever gestures are meaningful to you. Different people may think of different gestures. So for Surat al-Fatihah, we might recite:

- Maliki yaum id-din ("Master of the Day of Judgement"). Think of a gesture expressing this, e.g. pointing forwards to show that the Day of Judgement is in the future for everyone.
- Iyyaka nabudu wa iyyaka nastain ("It is You we worship, and upon You we call for help"). Think of a gesture such as offering hands forward to show that we praise God, and then the reverse to show that we hope for help in return.

Concentrate on the postures

While various of the things we say during salah are optional, all the postures are obligatory. We should therefore concentrate on making the postures accurately. For instance, in bowing (ruku), the back should be straight and parallel to the floor. One way of thinking of this is to imagine a glass of water on your back. You should not bow so much that the water would spill onto your head. Nor should you bow so little that the water would spill towards your legs.

Vary how you perform prayers

Adding variety to the way you perform your prayers allows us to get away from the routine that destroys concentration. There are only four things that you must say during salah, for it to be valid: (i) takbir (*Allahu Akbar* at the start), (ii) Surat al-Fatihah, (iii) the shahadah (the declaration of faith, when seated), (iv) the salam, right and left, to close the prayer.

Everything else is optional, such as short surahs or passages from the Quran or duas praising the Prophet, and may or may not be said.

Recite surahs after Al-Fatihah

Muslims all know at least a few of the shorter surahs from the end of the Quran. Reciting them after Al-Fatihah breaks up the routine of salah prayers. It may also help in remembering which rakaah we are performing. And we can always memorize more than just a few short surahs. Muhammad said: "He in whose heart there is no part of the Quran is like a deserted house" (At-Tirmithi).

In another At-Tirmithi hadith, Muhammad said: "The key to Paradise is prayer, and the key to prayer is ablution." This shows that prayer is very important in Islam, as all Muslims know. However, the choice of ablution (wudu) as the key to prayer may strike readers as unexpected.

If Muslims perform wudu perfectly with concentration, and not absent-mindedly, it is likely that they will maintain this concentration in the actual prayer that follows. The techniques suggested in this chapter all aim at avoiding a wandering mind and absent-mindedness in prayer.

1 Imam Shafii (820). *Kitab al-umm* ("The exemplar"). https://pdf.wecabrio.com/kitab-al-umm-english-translation.pdf

8 Fasting "as it was prescribed for those before you"

In the Quran (2:183), God (Allah) says: "O you who believe! Fasting is prescribed for you, as it was prescribed for those before you, that you may become righteous." This is the verse that obliges Muslims around the world (one quarter of mankind) to fast during Ramadan.

The next chapter describes the many benefits that accrue from fasting. This chapter concentrates on the phrase "as it was prescribed for those before you", referring to fasting in other religions.

Definition

First, we need to clarify what the word *fast* means, taking care not to confuse it with the sense meaning "quick" or "quickly".

In Islam, the fast of Ramadan is easily defined. It means to eat no food and consume no drink (as well as abstaining from other things such as sexual relations) from dawn (the beginning of the Fajr prayer period) to sunset (the beginning of the Maghrib prayer period). The length of the fast each day may vary according to your location and the season. Fasting during Ramadan is compulsory on Muslims, provided they are old enough and fit enough. Fasting at other times is also encouraged. The emphasis on fasting in Islam is shown in a hadith recorded by An-Nasai, when Prophet Muhammad (pbuh) was asked: "Which is the best deed?", and he replied: "Fasting, for there is nothing equal to it."

Let us see whether this Muslim definition corresponds to what is contained in English dictionaries.

Muslims around the world perform the fast of Ramadan in exactly the same way. They may eat different types of foods and consume different drinks before and after the fast, but the fast is the same. There are thus probably more Muslims fasting than in any other religion. This is probably the reason that dictionaries use the Muslim fast in Ramadan in illustrative sentences, rather than other religions.

> *Muslims fast during Ramadan.* (Longman)
>
> *The fast is broken at sunset, traditionally with dates and water.* (Collins)
>
> *... the Muslim holy month of fasting and prayer.* (Collins)

Several dictionaries give the Muslim definition of fasting, namely as a 100% ban on food (although they overlook drink).

> To eat no food for a period of time (Cambridge)
>
> To abstain from all food (Dictionary.com)
>
> Fasting is going for a certain length of time without eating anything. (Vocabulary.com)
>
> A period during which someone does not eat, especially for religious reasons (Longman)
>
> If you fast, you eat no food for a period of time, usually for either religious or medical reasons, or as a protest. (Collins)
>
> To abstain from food (Merriam-Webster)
>
> To abstain from food (American Heritage Dictionary)

However, the definitions given in some dictionaries add some hedging to this 100% ban, even in dictionaries that give a 100% ban in their definition.

> Abstain from all or some kinds of food or drink, especially as a religious observance. (Oxford)
>
> Abstinence from food or drink or both for health, ritualistic, religious, or ethical purposes. (Britannica)
>
> To eat only sparingly or of certain kinds of food, especially as a religious observance. (Dictionary.com)
>
> To eat little or no food for a period of time, especially for religious reasons (Longman)
>
> To eat sparingly or abstain from some foods (Merriam-Webster)
>
> To eat no food or very little food for a period of time, often for religious reasons (Macmillan)
>
> To eat very little or abstain from certain foods, especially as a religious discipline. (American Heritage Dictionary)

Muslims would argue that anything other than a 100% ban is dieting rather than fasting.

Fasting in other religions

The remainder of this chapter briefly describes fasting practices in other religions. As we shall see, fasting is part of the doctrine and practices of major world religions, with two exceptions.

Hinduism

The Sanskrit word for fasting in Hinduism is *upavasa*. Its literal meaning is "staying near the Lord". It is the origin of the Malay/Indonesian word *puasa* "fast" found in Malaysia, Singapore, Brunei and the world's largest Muslim country, Indonesia.

However, there is large variation in how, when and why Hindus fast, based on personal beliefs and local customs. "Most devout Indians fast regularly or on special occasions like festivals. On such days they do not eat at all, eat once or make do with fruits or a special diet of simple food."[1]

If followed strictly, the person fasting does not partake of any food or water from the previous day's sunset until after the following day's sunrise – in short, mostly when you are asleep. In fact, this is the origin of the English word *breakfast*, meaning eating after having not eaten since the last meal of the previous day. Fasting in Hinduism can also mean limiting oneself to one meal during the day and/or abstaining from eating certain food types and/or eating only certain food types. Practices vary widely in the different states of India, and in Indian communities around the world.

Judaism

Fasting in Islam is very similar to fasting in Judaism.

Yom Kippur (the Day of Atonement, 10th Tishri) is the last of 10 days of repentance. It is forbidden on that day to eat, drink, wash, wear leather, or have sexual relations. In addition, prohibitions on working, similar to those on the Sabbath, are enforced.

It should also be noted that Moses (Musa) fasted according to the Torah: "And he was there with the Lord 40 days and 40 nights; he neither ate bread nor drank water" (Exodus 34:28).

While Yom Kippur is the only fast commended in Judaism, there are a large number of other optional fasts, the majority of which commemorate deaths, destruction and sieges in the history of the ancient Jews[2,3].

Christianity

Catholics observe Lent, which is a fast of the 40 days leading up to Easter, starting with what is known as Ash Wednesday, and ending on Easter Sunday. It commemorates the 40-day fast of Jesus (Isa), who is recorded in the gospels to have fasted like Moses: "And he fasted 40 days and 40 nights and afterwards he was hungry" (Matthew 4:2 and Luke 4:2).

However, many Christians regard fasting as a personal choice rather than a commandment from God. Thus, many Christians do not fast. This is despite the fact that there are many examples in the Jewish, Hebrew Old Testament describing individuals fasting. There are also references to fasting in the Greek New Testament.

The Pharisees in Jesus's time fasted regularly, and asked Jesus why his disciples did not. Jesus answered them using a parable (Luke 5:33-39, Matthew 9:14-15, Mark 2:18-20).

"And he [Jesus] said unto them [disciples]: 'This kind [of demon] can come forth [i.e. be exorcised] by nothing, but by prayer and fasting'" (Mark 9:29).

Buddhism

We stated at the start that there are two world religions that do not involve fasting. It is not a prominent feature of Buddhism, and it is absent from Sikhism.

In Buddhist countries like Thailand, monks and nuns following the Vinaya rules walk through the streets each day with bowls to allow people to give food and thereby earn merit. The monks and nuns commonly eat this as the noon meal, and do not eat again after this.

However, many orders today do not enforce this. It is not considered a fast, but rather a means for monks to attain the discipline required for meditation, and for lay people to gain merit by giving.

Buddhist lay people generally look on fasting as asceticism. They do not generally fast, considering it a deviation from the Middle Way.

Sikhism

The Sikh Gurus discourage the devotee from engaging in this ritual as it is considered to "bring no spiritual benefit to the person". The Sikh holy scripture, Sri Guru Granth Sahib, tells us: "Fasting, daily rituals, and austere self-discipline - those who keep the practice of these, are rewarded with less than a shell."[4]

So most Buddhists and Sikhs have never undertaken a fast of any kind.

In Islam, all the major rules regarding fasting are laid down in the Quran and hadith. As a result, Muslims are in no doubt about what they must and must not do during Ramadan. The great advantage of this is that Muslims believe they are doing precisely what God wants them to do, and Muslims can fast in confidence, regardless of the country they may find themselves in.

1 Saranam.com (2023). *Fasting.* https://www.saranam.com/cms/170/Fasting.htm

2 Greenstone, J. H., Hirsch, E. G. & Hirschfeld, H. (2021). Fasting and fast-days. *Jewish Encyclopedia.* https://www.jewishencyclopedia.com/articles/6033-fasting-and-fast-days

3 Miller, D. (2016). A few facts about fasting in Jewish tradition. *My Jewish Learning.* https://www.myjewishlearning.com/2016/10/04/a-few-facts-about-fasting-in-jewish-tradition

4 Sri Guru Granth Sahib (n.d.). *Sri Granth.* https://www.srigranth.org/servlet/gurbani.gurbani?S=y (p. 216, line 5)

9 The deeper meaning of fasting

Why do Muslims fast? The simple answer is that God (Allah) states in the Quran (2:183): "O you who believe! Fasting is prescribed for you, as it was prescribed for those before you, that you may become righteous." Three points need to be made with regard to this verse.

Firstly, "Fasting is prescribed for you" means that it was prescribed by the revelation of this verse. That is, from that time on, Muslims must fast.

Secondly, as we have seen in Chapter 8, there is nothing new about fasting, or anything specific to Islam. Almost all world religions entail fasting for their adherents. Whether the adherents follow this requirement or not is another matter.

Thirdly, the final part states: "[so] that you may become righteous." The Arabic word here is *taqwa*, translated variously as "righteousness, piety, fear of God, God-consciousness, love for God, self-restraint". The purpose of fasting is thus to become closer to God, and as a prerequisite for all the other things that Muslims are expected to do during Ramadan: remembrance of God (thikr), reading the Quran, extra prayers, charity, etc. The purpose is not so that you feel hungry and thirsty.

Note also that the Quran states: "[so] that you *may* become righteous", the hedging of the English *may* expressed by the Arabic *la*. It does not say: "[so] that you *will* become righteous." Although fasting is an important form of worship, Ramadan still offers deeper opportunities which every believer should strive to explore.

In many countries, Ramadan is referred to as "the fasting month". This is true: Muslims fast in Ramadan. However, fasting is the bare minimum. This chapter examines the various levels of fasting, from basic to advanced. The more levels Muslims fulfil, the greater the likelihood that they will attain taqwa.

The ritual level

This can be considered the entry level, as it fulfils the religious requirement, but no more than that. Muslims should fast unless they are young (taken to be about ten years old, although children may perform partial fasts before this), ill, pregnant or breastfeeding, elderly, senile, or traveling. The fast involves giving up food, drink, and sexual intercourse between dawn and sunset for the month of Ramadan, which is 29 or 30 days long, because it is a lunar month.

Merely fulfilling the ritual level "ticks the box".

A Muslim should try to incorporate as many of these levels as possible, and complete the other activities that should occur in Ramadan, such as performing extra prayers, reading the Quran, giving charity, and avoiding backbiting and lying. As Prophet Muhammad (pbuh) said: "Perhaps a fasting person will gain nothing but hunger and thirst" (Ibn Majah).

The physical level

Muhammad used to eat a light meal (*sahur*) before dawn. At sunset, he would break his fast with dates and a glass of water, before leading the sunset prayer (Maghrib). He would then eat a moderate meal.

He warned his followers against eating too much. In a hadith, he stated:

> The worst container a human being can fill is his stomach. A few morsels of food to keep a person's back straight are sufficient. However, if his desire overcomes him, then let him eat a third, drink a third and leave a third for breathing (Ibn Majah).

In short, you should never eat until your stomach is full. And Ramadan is about fasting, not feasting.

Following Muhammad's example means that you experience hunger and thirst, and thus develop empathy with the millions around the world who do not have enough to eat and drink.

Fasting has several physical benefits. Fasting encourages the endorphin neurotransmitter system, related to the feeling of wellbeing and euphoria, to produce more endorphins and makes us feel better. It is similar to the high we can get from exercise.

During a fast, the body uses up stored cholesterol (fat) that is often deposited in the blood system, as well as in other fatty areas of the body. Thus it helps to keep the body firm and reduces the risk of heart attacks.

When breaking their fast, Muslims may celebrate completing a day's fasting, and successfully fulfilling a religious duty. However, they should also remember that there are plenty of poor people in the world who do not have enough food and water, and they should be thankful.

The libidinal level

Ramadan is famous for giving up food and drink. However, sexual activities with your spouse must also be given up, from dawn to sunset. Fasting helps in this respect, in that it reduces sexual desires.

Being able to restrain oneself during Ramadan is a large step towards conquering your lower desires (nafs). Muhammad said: "O youths, whoever among you is able to marry, let him do so, for it restrains eyes and protects the private parts. He who is unable to marry, should fast, because it is a shield" (Bukhari, Muslim).

The emotional level

Al-Ghazali, the 12th-13th century CE scholar, wrote: "Three habits destroy a man or woman: greed, envy and pride." He emphasized that envy leads to greed, and greed leads to anger. Similarly, pride is the exact opposite of what Islam teaches. Rather, we should aim for humility, as mentioned in many hadiths of Muhammad. For instance, he said: "Indeed, humility increases the dignity of one endowed with it. Be humble, and Allah will exalt you" (Muslim). Al-Ghazali spent much of his life studying positive virtues such as patience, thankfulness, and generosity, as well as negative vices such as suspicion, arrogance, ignorance, and jealousy. These are the personal qualities that we should be working on during Ramadan.

Anger is one of the most detrimental emotions, and the month-long fasting during Ramadan can help us to avoid losing our temper. Muhammad said: "When one of you is fasting, he should abstain from indecent acts and unnecessary talk, and if someone begins an obscene conversation or tries to start an argument, he should simply tell him, 'I am fasting'" (Bukhari, Muslim).

It is often difficult to stay calm in conversation, especially when you are sure you are in the right. However, it is better to exercise patience and let it drop, thus keeping your emotional fast intact.

The psychological level

Ramadan allows the Muslim the opportunity to take control of psychological thoughts and the actions that follow on from them. Failure to do so may lead to one's fast being null and void. Muhammad said: "Allah has no need for the hunger and the thirst of the person who does not restrain himself from telling lies and acting on them even while observing the fast" (Bukhari).

The modern world is characterized by immediate gratification. The difference between immediate gratification and delayed gratification is patience (sabr). While fasting, Muslims learn to be patient, and realize the benefits that derive from it.

During Ramadan, life still goes on and Muslims need to go to work, university, and school. However, Ramadan forces us to be more diligent in performing prayers on time during these busy times. And at other times (evenings, weekends), we need to remember God and the Hereafter, with extra prayers, thikr, reading the Quran, and so on. For one month, we can put the temporal pleasures of this world on hold.

Food has become a major part of modern life for many people. We often take a break and have a cup of tea and a snack. However, Ramadan shows us that we can live perfectly well without these. Fasting means changing our daily eating habits, eating a meal before dawn and at sunset, but nothing in between. The pre-dawn meal is known as *sahur*, and the sunset meal breaking the fast is *iftar*. We therefore learn the psychological control over the usual desire to eat or drink something.

The spiritual level

As mentioned in the hadith at the beginning of this chapter, the purpose of fasting in Ramadan is to attain righteousness, God-consciousness (taqwa). We are now entering the spiritual level.

Muhammad said: "Indeed, the reward of deeds depends on the intentions, and each person will be rewarded according to what he intended" (Bukhari, Muslim). Intention (*niyah* in Arabic) is thus a vital part of any action, including fasting. That is why Muhammad made it a requirement to declare the intention at the beginning of each day in Ramadan. "Whoever does not intend to fast before Fajr [dawn] will have no fast" (Abu Daud).

This daily repetition of the intention establishes a spiritual foundation of sincerity. In several hadiths, Muhammad emphasized the great rewards that may come from sincere fasting for the sake of God.

> "Whoever fasts Ramadan out of sincere faith and seeking reward from God, his previous sins will be forgiven" (Bukhari).
>
> "From one Ramadan to the next is atonement for the sins between them" (Muslim).

Muhammad described a gate in Paradise (Jannah) called Rayyan that is reserved for those who fast. He also highlighted how it has been made easier for Muslims to gain Paradise during Ramadan. "When Ramadan comes, the gates of Paradise are opened, the gates of Hell are closed, and the devils are chained" (Bukhari, Muslim).

Of the five pillars of Islam, Ramadan is the only one that cannot be seen by others. We can see and hear someone making the declaration of faith and performing prayers, paying zakah to someone, and going on Hajj. However, you can see if someone is not fasting, but cannot see if someone is fasting. A person's fast is a matter between them and God. God was quoted by Muhammad as saying: "Every act of Adam's descendants is for themselves, except fasting. It is meant for Me alone, and I alone will give the reward for it" (Muslim).

A Muslim may fast during Ramadan and do nothing else, and this fulfils the minimum requirement. However, for Ramadan to be an experience each year in which the Muslim attempts to attain righteousness, the other levels are necessary in order to transform them from within. At the end of each Ramadan, a Muslim should feel revitalized spiritually, and this should be shown in their subsequent, changed character and behavior (adab).

This chapter is based on a pamphlet written by Dr. Bilal Philips for the Qatar Guest Centre.

10 The different types of charity in Islam

In Section 4, we make the point that there are many Islamic concepts, and thus Arabic terms, that cannot be satisfactorily translated into English. One such concept is charity.

An English dictionary typically defines *charity* as "the act of giving money, food, or other kinds of help to people who are poor, sick, etc."[1] Nobody would argue with this general definition of the word *charity*. However, in Islam there are three very distinct types of charity.

Zakah

Zakah is one of the major religious duties in Islam and is the third of the five pillars of Islam. The literal meaning of zakah is "purification" and "growth". Zakah refers to the purification of a believer's wealth and soul. When we give, God multiplies our wealth and therefore not only are we purifying our wealth, we are also growing it with God's mercy. Zakah is what a believer returns out of his or her wealth to the neediest of Muslims for the sake of God.

There are two types of zakah, both of which are obligatory annually on Muslims: zakat al-fitr and zakat al-mal.

Zakat al-fitr

The following hadith relates to zakat al-fitr: "Muhammad enjoined the payment of one sa' of dates or one sa' of barley as zakat ul-fitr on every Muslim, slave or free, male or female, young or old, and he ordered that it be paid before the people went out to offer the Eid [ul-Fitr] prayer" (Bukhari*)*.

Several points are contained in this (and other, similar) hadiths:

Zakat al-fitr is obligatory (enjoined).

The amount is specified. One sa' is about three kilograms. The equivalent value of one sa' of dates or barley (or other staples such as meal, cottage cheese, raisins, as mentioned in other hadiths) can be made in money. It is a small amount, less than US$15.

It is obligatory on every Muslim. The head of a household may make the payment on behalf of his dependents.

Zakat al-fitr must be made during Ramadan, before Eid prayer on the first day of the next month (1 Shawal, Eid ul-Fitr). As compulsory fasting and zakat al-fitr both take place during Ramadan, they are often mentioned together. Prophet Muhammad (pbuh) said: "The fasting of the month of fasting will be hanging between Earth and heavens, and it will not be raised up to the divine presence without paying the zakat al-fitr" (An-Nasai).

Zakat al-mal

Zakat al-mal is payable on your savings and wealth. Again, there are precise specifications, contained in various hadiths.

Zakah is only compulsory on Muslims that are of legal age.

Zakah is paid on the remaining savings after a Muslim has spent on basic necessities, family expenses, loans and taxes. Zakah cannot be set off against the tax you pay to the government.

Zakat al-mal is an obligation on every Muslim, male or female, who possesses the minimum threshold (nisab in Arabic). Muhammad said: "No zakah is due on property amounting to less than five uqiyas [of silver, roughly 32 dinars], and no zakah is due on fewer than five camels, and there is no zakah on less than five wasqs [roughly 900 kg of staple food]" (Bukhari). The threshold of gold is 87.48g (Hanafi) and 84.7g (Shafii) of pure gold. The threshold of silver is 612.36g (Hanafi) and 592.9g (Shafii) of pure silver. The threshold of other kinds of money and currency is to be scaled to that of the value of gold. Local Islamic authorities should be able to clarify the precise amount.

Zakat al-mal is calculated at 2.5% (one fortieth) of the applicable amount, regardless of its size.

The Muslims to whom zakat al-mal and zakat al-fitr can be given (eight asnaf) are specified by God in the Quran (9:60):

> Charities are for the poor, and the destitute, and those who administer them, and for reconciling hearts, and for freeing slaves, and for those in debt, and in the path of God, and for the traveler in need – an obligation from God.

Zakat al-mal can be paid at any time during the Islamic lunar year. However, many Muslims find it convenient to pay it during Ramadan, for two reasons. Firstly, it can be paid at the same time as zakat al-fitr, which must be paid during Ramadan. Secondly, the rewards for any kind of charity – obligatory or voluntary – during Ramadan are greater than during the rest of the year. In a hadith, Muhammad said: "Ramadan is an honorable and blessed month, and the rewards for generosity are multiplied in it" (At-Tirmithi).

While zakat al-fitr is a small amount, less than US$15, the amount of zakat al-mal due depends on the size of the wealth of the Muslim. It may amount to hundreds, or thousands of dollars. Nevertheless, it is obligatory, just as zakat al-fitr is obligatory, in order to purify wealth.

Sadaqah

Sadaqah, which is usually also translated into English as "charity", is any charity that is not zakat al-fitr or zakat al-mal. There are various points that should be remembered when giving sadaqah.

The purpose of giving sadaqah

In the Quran, God reminds us that the purpose of giving charity is to hope for rewards from Him.

> Those who spend their wealth for increase in self-purification, and have in their minds no favor from anyone for which a reward is expected in return, but only the desire to seek for the countenance of their Creator most High; and soon will they attain [complete] satisfaction" (92:18-21).

Similarly, Uthman ibn Affan, the third caliph, said: "Your charity is not accepted until you believe 'I need the reward more than the beggar needs the money.'"

Sadaqah is not necessarily monetary

Sadaqah is a voluntary act of charity which is not limited to giving out money from your wealth. Sadaqah can be any act of kindness (financial, in kind, or by actions) from which another person or animal benefits (see Chapter 1).

Donate your talents, skills and strengths

It is also sadaqah to give your talents, skills and strengths in helping the community and for good work. God has blessed each of us with different talents and if we all work together, we can build a better place.

Many Muslims absolve their obligation for charity only by donating lots of money during Ramadan to various causes. Although these are all noble acts, what about other lasting charity acts that we can do physically? Two hadiths show that this is charity too.

Muhammad said: "Every good deed is charity" (Bukhari).

He also said:

> On every person's joints or small bones [i.e. fingers and toes], there is sadaqah due every day when the Sun rises. Doing justice between two people is sadaqah; assisting a man to mount his animal, or lifting up his belongings onto it is sadaqah; a good word is sadaqah; every step you take towards prayer is sadaqah; and removing harmful things from pathways is sadaqah (Muslim).

Size is not so important

The amount involved in charity is not so important. What is important is the intention and regularity. Muhammad said: "Save yourself from Hellfire even by giving half a date-fruit in charity" (Bukhari).

In a Bukhari hadith (quoted in Chapter 2), Muhammad explained that God loves most those deeds that are consistent and regular, even if they are small.

Do not keep count of the sadaqah you give

You should give in sadaqah what you can afford to, without keeping a note of how much it was. Muhammad said: "Spend in charity and do not keep count, for then Allah will also keep count in giving you provision" (Bukhari, Muslim).

Do not make a show of giving sadaqah

In a Bukhari hadith, Muhammad said: "Seven people will be shaded by Allah under His shade on the day when there will be no shade except His." The sixth of the seven categories is: "a man who gives in charity and hides it, such that his left hand does not know what his right hand gives in charity."

God reinforces this in the Quran (2:270-271): "And whatever you spend in charity or whatever vow you make, be sure Allah knows it all. But the wrongdoers have no helpers. If you disclose [acts of] charity, even so it is well, but if you conceal them and make them reach those [really] in need, that is best for you. It will remove from you some of your [stains of] evil. And Allah is well acquainted with what you do."

Sadaqah must be from lawful (halal) sources

Whatever you give in sadaqah must have been acquired in a halal way. For example, gambling in a casino is haram in Islam. You cannot, therefore, win money at a casino and then expect to make this money halal by giving it away in charity.

It is better to give than to receive

In a Bukhari hadith, Muhammad said: "The upper hand is better than the lower hand." This means that the person who gives charity is better than the one who takes it. This does not mean that poor people should refuse charity. However, everyone should try to give some charity, regardless of the form or amount. A smile costs absolutely nothing.

Start with your dependents

Sadaqah can be given to anyone who needs it. However, the hadith just quoted continues with a reminder that charity begins at home. "One should start giving first to his dependents."

Do not delay giving sadaqah

In life, we can never be sure what will happen the next day, week, month, or year. It is therefore important to give charity whenever you can, and not to delay it until it is too late.

In the Quran (63:10), God reminds us of this:

> And give from what We have provided for you, before death approaches one of you, and he says, "My Lord, if only You would delay me for a short while, so that I may be charitable, and be one of the righteous."

Use kind words

A kind word can be sadaqah. When giving sadaqah, we should not insult the dignity of the recipient by unkind words, or reminding them of the favor we are doing. God emphasizes this in the Quran (2:264), pointing out that it may even nullify your charity: "Do not make your almsgiving void by taunting and hurting."

Embrace humility

God makes it clear in the Quran (31:18) that pride is not a Muslim characteristic: "And do not turn your cheek [in contempt] towards people and do not walk through the Earth exultantly. Indeed, God does not like every self-deluded and boastful person."

When giving zakah or sadaqah, it is important for the individual to reflect where the charity – whether in money, in kind, or by actions – comes from, and remind ourselves that all things, wealth, and abilities ultimately belong to God. We should therefore be appreciative for being able to give charity for His sake.

Ongoing charity

In a hadith recorded by Muslim, Muhammad said: "When a person dies, their deeds end except for three: ongoing charity, beneficial knowledge, or a righteous child who prays for them." Ongoing charity (*sadaqah jariyah*) refers to something that is done in either your name or that of a loved one who has passed on, whose benefits and thus rewards continue in both this world and the Hereafter, for as long as they are used. Examples include building a mosque, a school, a hospital, or a well.

The concept of charity is deeply rooted in the Islamic identity. In many places, the Quran and the hadiths remind us of this, whether it is by reminding us to feed the poor and provide for the needy, support orphans, relatives and travelers, or spend in the way of God. All of these references emphasize the importance of charity in a Muslim's life.

1 Britannica Dictionary (2023). *Charity*. https://www.britannica.com/dictionary/charity

11 Don't delay Hajj

The pilgrimage to Makkah (Hajj) is the last of the five pillars of Islam. Each year, around three million Muslims make their way to Saudi Arabia to perform the various acts that are required. By carrying out the same acts of worship in the same places at the same time, pilgrims are cheek by jowl with other pilgrims from other countries. By wearing the same basic clothes – for men, two pieces of toweling or cloth – pilgrims have the same appearance, whether rich or poor. What unites them all is that they are Muslims on Hajj fulfilling this pillar.

It is a truly transformative experience. Pilgrims return as changed people. This was felt keenly by Malcolm X, the US human rights activist, who was originally a vocal advocate for Black empowerment. He converted to Islam in prison in 1948, and performed Hajj in 1964. The experience changed his attitude towards white-skinned people.

> During the past eleven days here in the Muslim world, I have eaten from the same plate, drunk from the same glass, and slept on the same rug – while praying to the same God – with fellow Muslims, whose eyes were the bluest of blue, whose hair was the blondest of blond, and whose skin was the whitest of white. And in the words and in the deeds of the white Muslims, I felt the same sincerity that I felt among the black African Muslims of Nigeria, Sudan and Ghana. We were truly all the same (brothers) – because their belief in one God had removed the white from their minds, the white from their behavior, and the white from their attitude.[1]

All pilgrims have similarly uplifting stories to tell when they return.

There are various commitments that come into play in deciding when you should perform the Hajj pilgrimage. However, the overriding commitment is that, as God (Allah) says in the Quran, all Muslims should perform Hajj once in their lifetime. "Pilgrimage [Hajj] to this House [the Kabah] is an obligation by Allah upon whoever is able among the people" (3:97). Hajj is thus one of the pillars of Islam.

The expression "whoever is able" is taken to mean financial ability to pay for the travel, accommodation, etc.; physical ability to go to all the required places and perform the required acts; and mental ability to understand the significance of the rituals of Hajj.

Financial ability

Going on Hajj is not a cheap undertaking. Naturally, its cost depends on many factors: where in the world you live (and thus how far you have to travel to get to Saudi Arabia); whether you want to take in Madinah and Al-Quds (Jerusalem) (which are not obligatory) as well as Makkah; how many days you want to spend in Saudi Arabia; what accommodation you want to use; how close you want to stay to Masjid al-Haram and Masjid an-Nabawi.

Much of the cost relates to the airfare, and that depends largely on the distance. Pilgrims from Europe and the UK (e.g. London 5,000 km), the USA (e.g. New York 10,000 km, Los Angeles 13,500 km) and Australasia (e.g. Perth 10,000 km, Auckland 15,000 km) will be paying substantial airfares. Also, Hajj tours from these regions normally use reputable hotels, with corresponding costs.

Physical ability

It should be remembered that Hajj involves various obligatory activities in and around Makkah. There are two obligatory acts that involve some physical fitness.

Tawaf is the process of walking around the Kabah seven times, anti-clockwise. The word *tawaf* refers to the completion of seven circuits; each circuit is known in Arabic as a *shawt*.

When entering Masjid al-Haram, it is recommended to perform tawaf. In Makkah, you do tawaf; in any other mosque in the world, you do *tahiyat ul-masjid* (two optional rakaah of prayer) in place of the tawaf that you cannot do because you are not in Makkah.

How far do Muslims walk when performing tawaf? The answer to this depends on how far from the Kabah the Muslim is. During quiet periods (e.g. at night, outside the Hajj period) it may be possible to perform tawaf next to the Kabah, on the courtyard that surrounds it (the *mataf*). If so, then one circuit is about 80 meters (or yards), and the whole tawaf is about 560 meters. However, during the Hajj period, the whole courtyard is a sea of Muslims performing tawaf, and it may be impossible to be anywhere near the Kabah. If so, it is permissible to perform tawaf in the enclosed area of the mosque, and even on the roof. If one does tawaf at the back of the roof area, one circuit is about 720 meters, and the whole tawaf is thus about 5 km – ten times as far.

Similarly, *sa'i* involves walking (and, for men, jogging part of the way) between the small hills Safa and Marwa, within the Masjid al-Haram compound. This relates to the story of Hajar, the wife of Abraham (Ibrahim), running between the two hills in search of water for her baby son Ishmael (Ismail).

The hills are mentioned in the Quran (2:158): "Indeed, Safa and Marwa are among the symbols of Allah. So whoever makes Hajj to the House [Kabah] or performs Umrah – there is no blame upon him for walking between them."

The reasons for men to run, or jog, during sa'i are that Hajar ran while looking for water, and also it was the custom of Prophet Muhammad (pbuh) and his Companions.

The distance between the two hills is about 450 meters. The total distance for the completion of sa'i, starting at Safa, completing seven one-way trips, and ending at Marwa, is over 3 km.

It should also be remembered that the mataf and the sa'i area are nowadays covered in marble tiles, which may be hard to the touch of bare feet used to wearing shoes.

There are other activities in Makkah which, while not obligatory parts of Hajj, are nevertheless completed by many Muslims.

Jabal an-Nur ("Mount of Light", meaning revelation) is a mountain on the outskirts of Makkah. It contains the cave Hira, where Muhammad received the very first revelation of the Quran (96:1-5). Muslims can climb to the cave, which is near the top of the mountain. The mountain is 642 meters high.

Similarly, Jabal Thawr, also on the outskirts of Makkah, is where Muhammad and Abu Bakr hid when they left Makkah for the Hijrah migration to Madinah. Jabal Thawr is 1,650 meters high.

It should also be remembered that these climbs may need to be made in the heat of Saudi Arabia. In summer, temperatures can reach as high as 50°C (120°F).

In short, a reasonable level of physical fitness is required for many of the activities involved in Hajj.

Mental ability

Perhaps the most difficult obstacle to performing Hajj is the mental one.

Performing Hajj while you are still a child may not be the wisest, in that someone who has not yet reached maturity may not understand the deep significance of the travel to, and the rituals performed at, Makkah.

The more important mental obstacle is the frame of mind and attitude towards one's obligation to perform Hajj in one's lifetime. We have already seen that Hajj requires both significant financial ability and considerable physical ability. However, many Muslims are tempted to delay performing Hajj until retirement, for financial reasons. Young Muslims may be worried about a university education and student debt. They may then need the financial outlay to start a business, and concentrate on their career. They would no doubt like to buy a house with furniture and appliances, and a car, as soon as they can afford it. They may meet the love of their life and decide to get married. Then, children come along, and need to be fed, clothed, and educated. All of these situations come with financial outlays.

But, as we have seen above, Hajj requires physical fitness, and we can never be sure how long our fitness will last. In a famous hadith, Muhammad advises us: "Take advantage of five [things] before five [other things]: your youth before your old age, your health before your sickness, your wealth before your poverty, your free time before your busyness, and your life before your death" (Shuab al-Iman). These all remind us not to delay carrying out obligatory activities. If we wait until retirement before performing Hajj, will we be fit enough? Indeed, will we still be alive then?

We need to change our mindset, be more positive, and plan to complete Hajj while we still can. There is a saying in business circles: failing to plan is planning to fail. That is, without a plan, we are unlikely to complete what we want to do. So, here is a five-point plan:

Make the intention now. Make the intention right now to complete Hajj. Nobody knows when they will die. However, God starts rewarding us once we make the intention for good deeds.

Be determined. A vague or insincere intention is not good enough if we hope to receive rewards from God. We should be sincerely determined to visit God's sacred house.

Make an effective plan. Make a plan of how you intend to earn the money required in a halal way, and how you will save towards Hajj. Also, plan when you will be able to take the leave required to go on Hajj, and how your work, your family, and other commitments will be covered while you are in Saudi Arabia.

Be prepared for accountability. If we die before we complete Hajj, we can still say, "God! You know that I had a plan and made a continuous effort."

Target for as soon as possible. We should make our Hajj a #1 priority. Our plan may not be able to be carried out next year, the year after, and so on, because of our circumstances and life's commitments. However, we should always be asking: "What is stopping me from going on Hajj next year?"

As all Muslims are very aware, the five daily prayers (salah) are obligatory on Muslims. In a well-known Bukhari hadith, Abdullah asked Muhammad: "Which deed is the dearest to Allah?" He replied: "To offer the prayers at their early stated fixed times." In other words, it is recommended to offer salah as soon as is practical after the call to prayer (*athan*), and not to leave it until, for example, just before the following athan.

The same can be said of performing Hajj, another of the compulsory pillars of Islam. It is recommended to perform it as soon as you are able. This means as soon as you are an adult, and have the financial means to do so, and while you still have your health and physical strength. In a hadith recorded by Bukhari, Muhammad said that a person who performs Hajj properly will return as a newborn baby (free of all sins). Surely we do not want to miss this opportunity to be free of sins, by waiting too long to perform Hajj? Surely we do not want to be free of sins, only to die shortly afterwards, because of old age? Nobody knows when they will die, so it makes sense for all Muslims to plan to perform Hajj.

1 Malcolm X with Alex Haley (1964). *The autobiography of Malcolm X*. Random House.)

12 Tips for Hajj

The purpose of this chapter is to encourage readers to undertake their own Hajj pilgrimage. Many of the points apply equally to the lesser Umrah pilgrimage.

Preparation

Before you go, do attend lectures on the topic of Hajj. Most mosques organize these. They provide a good outline of what to expect, and explain the rituals required of pilgrims to perform Hajj successfully.

Check with the organizers to ensure that lectures are being given in a language you understand, or that a full translation will be given simultaneously. Check, too, that appropriate arrangements have been made for sisters to attend – some sisters may find themselves the other side of a curtain so they will be unable to see the speakers or the demonstrations. The arrangements for translation can be far from satisfactory in some mosques, especially on the sisters' side, so ask about this beforehand.

Do not expect to remember everything you are told at this point. It is unnecessary. When you are on Hajj, you will receive almost daily briefings from the leaders of the group you are traveling with. On that subject, pick a reputable agent to go with; ask around among your Hajji friends (who have completed Hajj) and discuss the service they received from the group they went with.

On Hajj itself, some pilgrims choose to carry leaflets or booklets to remind them of what they are required to do at any given point. One such book is *Pilgrimage in Islam: A Comprehensive Guide to Hajj*[1], although there are many such books on the market.

Keeping yourself well informed about what you should be doing at each step provides confidence and peace of mind that your Hajj will be performed correctly, and will therefore be accepted (*Hajj mabrur*), God willing, insha Allah.

Before traveling, ask your doctor what vaccinations would be advisable. So many people from every corner of the planet gathered in one place means that you can expect to come home with a bug of one kind or another. One returned Hajji named his infection "camel cough". If anything more serious occurs while you are still on Hajj, the Saudi healthcare system is good and should be able to take care of you.

Mistakes with the contents of your luggage should be avoided. One mistake is taking two sets of male Hajj clothing (*ihram* sheets). They are quite bulky and heavy, and one set would suffice. Don't pack too many books to read; a Quran is sufficient, either printed or loaded digitally onto your cellphone. There are good bookshops in Makkah and Madinah, and you may find yourself returning home with a mini-library.

In the mosque

Hajj is an experience that almost defies description. It is huge by any measure. Masjid an-Nabawi – Prophet Muhammad's mosque in Madinah – can accommodate three-quarters of a million worshipers under air-conditioned cover.

Each year, in excess of three million pilgrims visit the same sites at about the same time so you can expect massive crowds everywhere you go. The mosques in Madinah and Makkah are so big that during prayers, an appointed person near the middle of the mosques repeats the imam's words "Allahu akbar" ("God is Great") and "Rabbana lakal hamd" ("Our Lord! All praise is for you") during prayers, so people near the back can know for sure when to prostrate and so on.

Some sights may surprise or even shock you. At Masjid al-Haram, some women have been known to insist on taking wudu at the men's open-air wudu station just outside the mosque, unwilling to go downstairs to their own area. It's impossible to avoid seeing this when you are at the next tap to the person, so just remain focused on what you are doing.

Women beggars have been known to enter the men-only tent at Mina, and beggars generally are a problem. Sound advice is not to give to these "professional beggars" but to give instead to the mosque cleaners, hotel staff and others who work for a pittance in Madinah and Makkah. A few Saudi riyals enables them to buy their food for one day, for example.

Keep your cool

Despite checking in simultaneously as husband and wife, airlines still manage to seat couples separately on occasion. Then you will need to negotiate with fellow passengers to swap seats in order to be together. This is ironic considering the emphasis on women travelling on Hajj with their close family (*mahram*). On one such "seat swap", the first fellow pilgrim making the offer to a Sunni Muslim turned out to be a Shia Muslim with beautifully refined manners, so perhaps the moral there is not to rush to judge others.

Despite the purpose behind Hajj, not everyone gets along. At Mina one year, a fight was witnessed one night between two groups of Sunni and Shia brothers. Whether their Hajj was accepted, only God knows.

Sometimes cultural differences can be hard to understand for some people. On one occasion, an Indonesian couple smartly attired in batik and other traditional clothing were waiting for an elevator in a shopping mall next to Masjid al-Haram. The man spoke to his wife, saying that the European man next to them, also waiting for the elevator, must be a tourist. Maybe he forgot that Makkah is a city only Muslims can enter. Or maybe he couldn't get over a Muslim in jeans and T-shirt. It was a reminder of that trick question: What is Muslim dress? The answer, of course, is that there is none. Muslim dress is essentially anything that's loose-fitting and covers the private parts (*aurah*).

A word you will hear constantly in the context of Hajj is patience (*sabr*). You need plenty of it to cope with the crowds; half-hour queues for toilets, wudu and showers; travel hiccups; constant delays and hold-ups. Allow plenty of time for everything.

One good suggestion for protecting your wife from being jostled by other men during tawaf is to have your wife walk immediately in front of you and put your arms out stiffly on each side of your wife's shoulders so nobody can cross her path.

In crowds generally, hold your wife's (or mother's, or daughter's, or sister's) hand so you do not get parted. It can happen all too easily. If you follow, for example, the school (*mathhab*) of Imam Shafii, then you will need to use Hanafi rules of wudu for Hajj. This is permissible during Hajj and it allows you to hold hands for this purpose without breaking your wudu.

Sadly, crowds attract pickpockets – especially outside Masjid al-Haram in Makkah. Take all necessary precautions because they are expert at parting you from your valuables.

Most people are doing the best they can in the circumstances, but moving three million people around for a single purpose must be a logistical nightmare. So show some compassion for the officials, many of whom are part-time and do another job the rest of the year.

Aim for humility and concentration (khushu)

The advice when doing tawaf (circumambulating the Kabah in Makkah) is to refrain from talking as tawaf is an act of worship. Despite this, you will probably see people chatting, chanting in groups and even uploading photos and taking videos. It is disrespectful, to say the least – as indeed are all the cellphones ringing during prayers.

It is possible to do without cellphones for the entire trip. This may let you focus on Hajj better without the distractions a cellphone can offer, not to mention save you the expense of local SIM cards. Agreeing beforehand where to meet after prayers is one way to avoid the need for your cellphone.

On the ground floor it can get very crowded, so try the roof. Go at cooler times of the day, such as just before dawn. Just keep an eye out for fast-moving wheelchairs. If you are on the roof of Masjid al-Haram during the day, look up. If you are lucky, you may see birds of prey soaring on the thermals high above the Kabah.

There are many beautiful sights and you may wish to take photographs so you have a visual record of your Hajj. The authorities have become more relaxed about this in recent years but don't push your luck in places such as the grave of our Prophet in Masjid an-Nabawi. Men try to take photos through the grille at the grave. It is bad manners; anyway, there is nothing to see. Visiting his grave is not part of Hajj but it is considered highly desirable (*mustahab*) by the four main schools of thought to do so.

A good rule regarding photography is to do the necessary rites of Hajj, then discreetly get the camera out if time permits and the circumstances are appropriate. Remember, your primary intention at all times is to perform Hajj successfully.

Many people feel that the Prophet's Mosque, and Madinah generally, is one of the most beautiful, tranquil places on Earth. It's worth being outside the mosque at dawn and at dusk to watch the enormous umbrellas opening and closing. They surround the entire mosque.

Of course, the main beauty comes from within: the joy of being able to spend many hours in quiet contemplation and reflection.

After nearly every one of the five daily prayers in the mosque, you will hear a call to funeral (*janazah*) prayers. It is good to remain an extra few minutes to perform these (they are very short) because of the blessings bestowed upon those who pray for the dead. If you are very near the front row of Masjid an-Nabawi, near the imam, you may be able to follow the funeral out to the adjacent famous cemetery named Baqi, which is where some Companions and family members of the Prophet are buried.

Hajj is an incredible experience. Clichés such as "the trip of a lifetime" hardly begin to do it justice. Try to perform it while you are still reasonably fit because it is physically, mentally and spiritually demanding (see the previous chapter).

1 Huseyin Yagmur (2016). *Pilgrimage in Islam: A comprehensive guide to Hajj* (2nd edition). Tughra Books.

2

Signs of God (Allah)

Signs of God (Allah)

If you ask a Muslim what the miracle of their religion is, they will go to their bookshelf, take their miracle down, show it to you, and you can read it. It is the Quran. Muslims believe that the Quran is from God (Allah), that is, it is verbatim (word-for-word) the word of God.

Let us carry out a hypothetical experiment. Imagine that you were God, and that you were revealing the Quran part-by-part to Prophet Muhammad (pbuh), and you wanted people to believe that the Quran was a book from you (God). How would you convince people?

There are three types of assertion that argue strongly for something being a book from God.

Firstly, you could start by declaring that it is a book and has been written as a consistent work. The Quran is patently a book, in the limited sense that it is printed pages between covers. However, we need to ask whether it is a book in the sense of a coherent work in terms of content. The Quran refers to itself in several places as a book, e.g.: "This is the book in which there is no doubt, a guide for the righteous" (2:2).

So, the Quran refers to itself and calls itself a book. It also calls itself the Quran (about 70 times), e.g.: "And chant the Quran rhythmically" (73:4). The word *Quran* is related to the word *iqra*, the very first word of the Quran revealed to Muhammad. So, it means "recitation".

Secondly, you could declare that it is from you (God). By itself, this does not prove that it is from God, but at least the claim has been made. The Quran itself claims that it is from God, e.g.: "The revelation of the Book is from God, the Exalted in Might, the Wise" (45:2).

Thirdly, and most persuasively, you could include information that only you (God) know. There are two types of such information.

Muslims believe that God knows what will happen in the world. Predictions that turn out to be accurate show that the writer knows the future.

Several predictions in the Quran came true during the lifetime of Muhammad and his Companions. So, they could see that the Quran contained accurate predictions. Some are explained in Chapter 20 of Section 3.

Muslims believe that God created everything, and thus has total knowledge of the sciences such as physics, chemistry, biology, and geology. Inserting scientific facts that Muhammad and his Companions knew little about would thus show later generations that it was written by a higher power.

Many such facts are contained in the Quran, that is, facts that were only proven to be facts by scientists centuries later, and often in the 20th century CE. They are way beyond the basic level of scientific knowledge in Muhammad's time. These scientific facts relate to subjects including embryology, astronomy, and the structure of mountains[1]. This section contains six chapters on astronomy, and the structure of mountains.

1 Ibrahim, I. A. (1997). *A brief illustrated guide to understanding Islam* (2nd edition). Darussalam. https://www.islam-guide.com/frm-ch1.htm

13 The Big Bang

The Planck observatory

Planck was the name of an observatory launched by the European Space Agency[1] to study the cosmic microwave background. This is detectable radiation dating back to the Big Bang origin of the universe.

The satellite was named Planck after Max Planck, the 19th-20th century CE German theoretical physicist and originator of the quantum theory. He has had various other phenomena named after him: Planck time, Planck length, Planck mass, Planck units.

The 1,900 kg satellite was launched in 2009. After seven sky surveys, its helium coolant was used up and it was switched off. It still circles the Earth, in what is known as "graveyard orbit".

The major product of the observatory is a detailed map tracing the oldest light in the sky[2]. Its pattern confirms the Big Bang theory for the origin of the universe but subtle, unexpected details have required scientists to adjust some of their ideas.

The map reveals tiny variations in the cosmic microwave background, the faint glow of radiation that is left over from the earliest light to illuminate the cosmos.

The map shows tiny deviations from the average background temperature of -270°C, where blue is slightly cooler and red is slightly warmer. The cold spots are where matter was more concentrated and later collapsed under gravity to form stars and galaxies. Scientists say its mottled pattern is an exquisite confirmation of the Big Bang model for the origin and evolution of the universe.

The Planck data also suggested the universe is expanding at a slower rate than previously thought, and is thus slightly older than previously thought, at 13.8 billion years old. Subsequently, however, in 2016, scientists found that the universe is expanding 5% to 9% faster than previously thought.

The scientific details are very technical; interested readers should consult external references.

The results were published in 2013 in a *Guardian* newspaper article[3]. What is interesting is some of the comments on the *Guardian* website about this. One example is: "Exciting. Our children and grandchildren look forward to ever more wonderful discoveries. The religious fundamentalists won't like it though. They will go into deep denial mode." This illustrates the blinkered outlook of many westerners who equate religion with Christianity. Perhaps these findings are a problem for fundamental Christianity – the literal belief that God created the universe in six days, as told in Genesis chapter 1 – but they are in harmony with Islam and the Quran.

The Big Bang Theory in the Quran

If the Quran was written by God, and if God created the universe and was therefore present when the world began, this would be proved by including in the Quran evidence in the form of a description of how the world began. In the Quran, we have precisely this: "Do the disbelievers not see that the heavens and the Earth were one mass, and We tore them apart? And We made from water every living thing. Will they not believe?" (21:30).

Three scientific facts are given in this one verse:

1 "… were one mass, and We tore them apart". This of course is the Big Bang theory. At one time, the universe was one piece, which burst. The Big Bang theory was proposed in 1927 by Belgian priest Georges Lemaître.

2 "We made from water every living thing". The microscope was invented by Dutchman Antonie van Leeuwenhoek in the 17th century CE. This allowed scientists to examine very small – literally microscopic – details about living organisms. As a result, van Leeuwenhoek is known as "the Father of Microbiology". Subsequently, it was discovered that the majority of living cells are composed of water. The amount of water in the human body is about 60% by weight for an average adult, and about 70% for an average child. The precise percentage depends on various factors: age, sex, weight, health, water intake, etc. Different parts of the body have different percentages, from 90% for blood to 15% for bone and 4% for teeth.

3 "Do the disbelievers not see?" The Big Bang theory, and the water composition of life were not discovered by Muslims, but by non-Muslims, i.e. "disbelievers".

The expanding universe in the Quran

Furthermore, it was discovered, by American astronomer Edwin Hubble in 1929, that the universe is expanding. Hubble was another non-Muslim "disbeliever", after whom the Hubble Space Telescope is named. This expansion was discovered in an investigation measuring the redshift in color of near and far galaxies. The effect is similar to standing by a road as a car speeds past. The note gets higher as it approaches and lower as it goes away. The same happens with redshift but with the color of light waves rather than the note of sound waves.

The expanding universe is also mentioned in the Quran: "We constructed the universe with power, and We are expanding it" (51:47).

It is fascinating to imagine what the early Muslims thought when verses like this were revealed. One can picture desert Arabs looking up at the sky and wondering how it is "expanding". However, we should be grateful that their faith meant that they were obliged not to change a word of it, as they recognized it as the word of God.

1 European Space Agency (n.d.). *Planck*. https://www.esa.int/Enabling_Support/Operations/Planck

2 Amos, J. (2013). Planck satellite: Maps detail Universe's ancient light. *BBC News*, 21 March 2013. https://www.bbc.co.uk/news/science-environment-21866464

3 Sample, I. (2013). Planck telescope maps light of the big bang scattered across the universe. *The Guardian*, 21 March 2013. https://www.theguardian.com/science/2013/mar/21/planck-telescope-light-big-bang-universe

14 Life on Earth

The Earth contains a number of features, all of which have to be present at the same time for life as we know it to be possible. "Life as we know it" includes the many forms of plant and animal life, including human beings. This balance between many factors is therefore essential for human beings to be able to exist on Earth.

These factors divide into two main types: the position of the Earth relative to the Sun, and the Earth's rotation, both of which govern temperature; and the composition of the atmosphere, in particular the gases oxygen and carbon dioxide.

The position of the Earth

1 Distance of the Earth from the Sun

The Earth is about 150 million km from the Sun on average. Because the orbit of the Earth is not perfectly circular, this distance varies between 147 and 152 million km. This, however, is a relatively minor variation, and the average temperature of the Earth is not changed appreciably because of it. If, on the other hand, the distance between the Earth and the Sun were much greater than this, then temperatures on Earth would be much colder. Vice versa, if the distance were much smaller than this, then temperatures would be much warmer. In either scenario, life on Earth would not exist.

2 The inclination of the Earth

The Earth revolves around the Sun. Also, the Earth spins on its own axis, once every 24 hours, giving us day and night. However, the Earth's axis of rotation is not at right angles to its orbital plane of rotation around the Sun. Instead, it is at an angle of 23 degrees. As a result, parts of the Earth are slightly closer to the Sun and therefore warmer at certain times of year, and conversely slightly further and cooler at others. In other words, the Earth has seasons.

Is the 23-degree angle critical? If the inclination were more than 23 degrees, the variation between the seasons would be more extreme, leading to unbearably hot summers and unbearably cold winters. So, 23 degrees is the right angle for the pleasant alternation of the seasons to occur.

If the axis of the Earth's rotation were at right angles to the axis of rotation around the Sun, then there would be no seasons. Every time of year would have the same temperature and weather patterns.

3 Speed of rotation

At what speed does the Earth rotate on its own axis? It makes one rotation per day (24 hours). If we take as our reference point the Equator, which is the furthest point from the axis, the surface of the Earth rotates at 460 meters per second, or 1,670 kph. This is an ideal speed of rotation. If it were faster, gas molecules would disperse into space, and the Earth's atmosphere would disappear. On the other hand, if it were slower, the Earth's gravitational pull would cause gas molecules to be absorbed, and the atmosphere would disappear.

Gases in the atmosphere

The gases in the atmosphere, and thus contained in the air we breathe, have to be in the right proportions for the Earth and life on Earth to be sustained. There are four main gases in the atmosphere: nitrogen (78%), oxygen (21%), argon (0.93%) and carbon dioxide (0.04%). Nitrogen is known as a chemically unreactive or inert gas, that is, one that takes part in very few chemical reactions in specific conditions. Argon is one of the six gases (helium, neon, argon, krypton, xenon and radon), known as the noble gases, that are similarly chemically unreactive. It is fortunate that they are unreactive because, for instance, if they could react (take part in chemical reactions) easily, the oceans would turn into nitric acid.

1 Oxygen

Oxygen (chemical symbol O), however, is a reactive gas, that is, it takes part in chemical reactions easily. It is thus an important part of compounds such as water (H_2O) and carbon dioxide (CO_2), both vital for life on Earth.

Earth is the only planet known to have oxygen. And oxygen is an essential component of the air that humans and other animals breathe. In other words, Earth is the only planet known to have an atmosphere that can sustain human life.

The percentage of oxygen in the atmosphere is 21%. If it were higher, oxidation would occur more quickly, and rocks and metals would be eroded sooner. The Earth would erode, and life on Earth would be threatened. Vice versa, if the percentage of oxygen were lower, breathing would become more difficult. Also, less ozone (O_3) would be produced. The ozone layer in the atmosphere is essential for shielding the surface of the Earth from harmful ultraviolet rays, so a thinner ozone layer would also threaten mankind and other living beings.

2 Carbon dioxide

Carbon dioxide is present in the atmosphere in a small percentage (0.04%), but it plays a vital role in life on Earth. There is a continual recycling of oxygen and carbon dioxide by the two processes known as cellular respiration, and photosynthesis.

Cellular respiration is the technical term for breathing. Living creatures, including human beings, breathe in air, including oxygen, and the oxygen is used to break down foods for energy. Carbon dioxide is produced as a waste product. Vice versa, plants synthesize carbohydrate molecules from carbon dioxide and water, thereby converting light energy into chemical energy. Oxygen is produced as a waste material.

If the percentage of carbon dioxide were less, the amount of plant life, both on land and in the sea, would be reduced. Plant life is necessary as a food source for animals including humans. The acidity of oceans would also rise, because of an increase in the amount of bicarbonate. If the percentage of carbon dioxide were greater, chemical erosion of the land would occur, leaving an alkali residue in the oceans. The greenhouse effect would increase, making the surface of the Earth hotter.

In short, the position and movement of the Earth, and the composition of its atmosphere are both a matter of fine balances. If any of the above positions, speeds and percentages were different, life on Earth, including human life, would not be possible.

What is the probability of all the above positions, speeds and percentages being at exactly the right levels by chance?

In several places in the Quran, God (Allah) states explicitly that He is the Creator, and that He created the Earth and its atmosphere as a habitat for mankind, e.g. "O people! Worship your Lord who created you and those before you, that you may attain piety. He who made the Earth a habitat for you, and the sky a structure" (2:21-22).

15 Solar eclipses

As we saw in the previous chapter, there are several factors that need to be exactly right for life on Earth to be possible: the Earth's distance from the Sun, the inclination of the Earth, its speed of rotation, and the levels of gases in the atmosphere, especially oxygen and carbon dioxide. What are the chances that all these factors happened to be exactly right randomly?

Similar questions can be asked about eclipses. There are two types of eclipse for us on Earth: a lunar eclipse and a solar eclipse.

Lunar eclipse

A lunar eclipse happens in the night sky when the Sun, Earth and Moon are in a line, such that the Moon is in the shadow of the Earth. It is also informally called a "blood Moon" because the Moon, which is normally white because it reflects the rays of the Sun, turns a red color.

Solar eclipse

However, this chapter discusses the similar phenomenon of a solar eclipse, which is touched on in several places in the Quran and hadiths. A solar eclipse occurs during daylight when the Sun, Moon and Earth are in a line, such that for us observers on the Earth, the Moon blocks the Sun. Or, to put it another way, the Earth is in the shadow of the Moon.

It is an eerie experience, because the Earth becomes dark in the middle of the day. There are many reports that animals that are used to the daily routine of daylight followed by darkness become disoriented. Nocturnal insects, such as crickets and cicadas, begin their night calls[1]. Vice versa, daytime birds stop their birdsong during an eclipse. Because the Sun's rays are no longer reaching the surface of the Earth, temperatures can drop by as much as 3°C, and it has been reported[2] that the speed of winds can decrease by 15 kph or more.

In the time of Prophet Muhammad (pbuh), a solar eclipse occurred when one of his sons died. His son Ibrahim was born in 630 but, after the Battle of Tabuk in 632, he died at the age of 16 or 18 months. His death coincided with a solar eclipse, which many Muslims took as a miraculous sign, saying that the Sun was eclipsed in sadness over the death of Ibrahim. A hadith reports:

> The Sun eclipsed in the lifetime of Prophet Muhammad on the day when [his son] Ibrahim died. So the people said that the Sun had eclipsed because of the death of Ibrahim. Muhammad said: "The Sun and the Moon do not eclipse because of the death or life [i.e. birth] of someone. When you see the eclipse, pray and invoke Allah" (Bukhari).

In other words, Muhammad realized that this was a natural phenomenon under the control of God, as mentioned in the Quran (41:37): "And of His signs are the night and the day, and the Sun and the Moon. Do not bow down to the Sun, nor to the Moon, but bow down to God, Who created them both, if it is Him that you serve."

Circumstances that produce a solar eclipse

Solar eclipses are a very convincing sign of God, because they rely on several features whose occurrence together is beyond the realm of coincidence. On Earth, we see a solar eclipse as the circle of the Moon with a thin ring of brightness from the Sun (corona) at its circumference. Many features have to coincide for this to appear.

Firstly, while diagrammatic representations of an eclipse show the bodies fairly close together, they are of course at literally astronomical distances from each other. The Moon is roughly 384,400 km from the Earth, while the Sun is roughly 149.6 million km away. If the Moon were closer to the Earth, it would appear bigger to us and obliterate the Sun and its light, throwing the whole Earth into darkness. If the Moon were further away, it would appear smaller, and fail to blot out the brightness of the Sun. The same effects would happen if the Sun were further away or closer. So, the relative distances of the bodies from the Earth are important.

Secondly, the relative sizes of the bodies are equally important. The diameter of the Moon is roughly 3,475 km, about a quarter that of the Earth. The diameter of the Sun is roughly 1.4 million km, over a hundred times that of the Earth. If the Moon were larger, it would have the same effect as being closer to the Earth, namely of obliterating the Sun and its light and throwing the whole Earth into darkness. Vice versa, if the Moon were smaller, it would have the same effect as being further from the Earth, namely of failing to blot out the brightness of the Sun. Again, a smaller or larger Sun would produce the same effect. So, the Moon and the Sun have to be of the right size and at the right distance in order to cause an eclipse and corona. Any larger/smaller and/or any further/closer, and an eclipse would not take place.

The third feature that has to be in place for an eclipse to occur relates to the orbital planes; that is, the ring that the Earth describes in circling the Sun is almost – but not quite – in the same plane as that of the Moon circling the Earth.

If the Moon's orbital plane were exactly the same as the Earth's, there would be a solar eclipse every single month because the Moon would come between the Earth and Sun every month. Similarly, there would be a lunar eclipse (blood Moon) every month, as the Earth would come directly between the Moon and the Sun.

In fact, the Moon's orbital plane is inclined at an angle of about 5 degrees to that of the Earth, so its shadow at new Moon usually misses Earth. It is this inclination that gives us a new Moon rather than an eclipse each month.

It would be very disruptive to life on Earth if a solar eclipse occurred every month. With the 5-degree inclination, solar eclipses occur at least twice, and up to five times, per year. The disorientation to life and weather on Earth caused by these infrequent eclipses has already been mentioned.

Finally, eclipses can be total or partial. In total eclipses, the Moon completely obliterates the disk of the Sun, leaving only a ring of corona light around the circumference. This causes darkness during the daytime, temperatures drop, and the natural world is disrupted. However, total eclipses only occur in relatively small areas of the surface of the Earth, because the Moon is not large enough for its shadow to cover the whole of the Earth. It is much more frequent for people to observe partial eclipses, where larger areas of the Earth's surface are covered by the penumbra, i.e. the partial shadow of the Moon. That is, for people in those areas, the Moon only covers part of the disk of the Sun, resulting in a substantial amount of sunlight still reaching the Earth's surface in those areas, and life being disrupted far less.

Because of the 5-degree inclination, the area of the Earth that is affected by a total eclipse is never the same. For this reason, eclipse-watchers travel to those areas where a total eclipse is calculated to occur.

There are many factors that have to be in place for a solar eclipse to be visible to us on Earth:

1. The Moon and Sun must be at the right distances relative to each other.
2. The Moon and Sun must be the right sizes relative to each other. As a result of #1 and 2, a ring of light (corona) is left around the circumference.
3. The Moon must be in a similar (but not quite equal) orbital plane to that of the Earth. Otherwise, there would be a solar eclipse every month.
4. The Moon's shadow must not be so large that it completely obliterates the Sun's light from the whole of the Earth's surface. Otherwise, it would be very disruptive to life on Earth.

Non-believers will tell us that natural occurrences like this are the result of random coincidence. However, the number of factors that have to be exactly right for a solar eclipse to occur is so many and so complex that this is beyond the realms of coincidence.

Muslims turn to the words of God as contained in the Quran (29:61) and have a simple answer: "And if you asked them, 'Who created the heavens and the Earth and regulated the Sun and the Moon?' they would say, 'God.' Why then do they deviate?" The Sun, Moon and Earth were created by God and these factors are designed to give us occasional, total or partial solar eclipses.

1 Thompson, T. (n.d.). Observing wildlife reactions during a total solar eclipse. *Eclipse-chasers*. https://www.eclipse-chasers.com/article/papers/wildlife01.html

2 Belles, J. (2019). The effects of a solar eclipse on the weather and what we learned from 2017. *The Weather Channel*. https://weather.com/science/space/news/2019-06-28-solar-eclipse-weather-argentina-chile-july-2

16 The Moon

The next three chapters (16 – 18) were all originally written by members of the Auckland-based Young Muslim Women's Association (YMWA). They organize activities to strengthen their bonds of sisterhood, to keep fit, and to appreciate the wonders of nature. In Islam, these marvels would be known as ayat ullah, signs of God (Allah).

New Zealand is a perfect country to do this, as it is well known for its scenery. After one such camping holiday, YMWA members wrote about three such signs: the Moon, stars, and mountains. All of these are visible to us, if we leave our houses and cities, and venture into the countryside. They would have been more obvious to the original Muslims, Prophet Muhammad (pbuh) and his Companions, who lived in the Arabian desert.

This chapter expresses wonder at the Moon, and relates this to several verses in the Quran.

The Moon is a very important element in Islam, as the religion uses a lunar calendar, and the sighting of the new Moon therefore determines significant dates in the calendar.

Etymology

It may not be obvious that, in English-speaking countries that do not use the lunar calendar, the words *month* and *Moon* are related. If instead of *month*, the English word were spelled *moonth*, i.e. the extent of one Moon, that would be obvious. The same is true in many other languages of countries that do not use the lunar calendar: the words for "month" and "Moon" are the same (given here in Roman alphabet transliteration, where necessary):

> Czech *měsic*, Estonian *kuu*, Hawaiian *mahina*, Igbo *ọnwa*, Indonesian/Malay *bulan*, Korean *dal*, Mandarin *yue*, Maori *marama*, Mongolian *cap*, Romanian *lună*, Swahili *mwezi*, Tagalog *buwan*, Tamil *tingal*, Turkish *ay*, Zulu *inyanga*.

In other languages, the words for "Moon" and "month" (and perhaps also "Monday") are not identical but closely related, e.g. German *Mond, Monat, Montag.*

Festivals

The Islamic lunar calendar consists of 12 months, each of 29 or 30 days. A new month is declared when the new Moon is sighted. The Islamic lunar year is thus about 11 days shorter than the Gregorian year (January, February, etc.). One benefit of this is that Islamic festivals do not become inextricably associated with particular times of year.

There are only two major festivals in the Islamic calendar: Eid ul-Fitr, and Eid ul-Adha.

Muslims make an effort to look for the new Moon at the end of the eighth lunar month of Shaban, looking forward to the beginning of the ninth month of Ramadan, with its fasting and other devotional activities (see Chapters 8 and 9). Then at the end of Ramadan, the new Moon signifies the end of Ramadan, and the start of the tenth month of Shawal. The first day of Shawal is Eid ul-Fitr, a day of celebration.

The second festival is Eid ul-Adha (literally "Festival of the sacrifice"). This celebrates two events: the submission of Prophet Abraham (Ibrahim) when he was tested to sacrifice his son Ishmael (Ismail); and the maybe 3 million pilgrims fulfilling their Hajj obligation. Eid ul-Adha is the 10th day of Thu al-Hijjah, the 12th month. The climax of Hajj is the Day of Standing at Arafat, on the 9th. It is therefore important that the new Moon indicating the start of the month of Thu al-Hijjah is sighted correctly.

Fasting

Fasting the 29 or 30 days of Ramadan is compulsory on all Muslims capable of doing so. As detailed in Chapter 2, it is also encouraged to perform voluntary fasts at other times. The start and end of Ramadan (like all lunar months) are determined by sighting the new Moon, although many countries nowadays do this by calculation.

Day and night

In various places in the Quran, God reminds us of the regularity of the movement of the Sun and Moon, under His control, giving us night and day.

"The Sun and the Moon move according to plan" (55:5).

"And He committed the Sun and the Moon to your service, both continuously pursuing their courses, and He committed the night and the day to your service" (14:33).

"It is He who created the night and the day, and the Sun and the Moon; each floating in an orbit" (21:33).

"By the Sun and its radiance, and the Moon as it follows it, and the day as it reveals it, and the night as it conceals it" (91:1–4).

When the Moon comes out, our body gets ready for rest. When the night falls, no matter how much we want to keep awake, it is unnatural for the body to feel at ease, keeping awake at nighttime. On those nights when the body does keep awake, it looks forward to resetting its body clock once more, to sleep at night. In the Quran, God reminds us (37 times) of the alternation between night and day, and that the night is for sleep, and the day for work, e.g. (25:47): "And it is He who made the night a covering for you, and sleep for rest; and He made the day a revival."

Splitting the Moon

During the time of Prophet Muhammad (pbuh), Allah showed a miracle by splitting the Moon into two. This was to prove to the people that there will be a Day of Resurrection. There was a moment when the Moon was split into two, which the onlookers witnessed with their own eyes. However, those who were stubborn refused to believe this and tried to pass it off as magic.

"The Hour has drawn near, and the Moon was split in two. Yet, whenever they see a sign, they turn away, saying: 'Same old magic'" (54:1–2).

The Moon was then brought back together by God proving that He is the one with power. Resurrection is just as easy for him.

"When We intend for something to happen, We say to it: 'Be', and it becomes" (16:40).

This same Moon that we see as regularly as clockwork every night will also be ordered to do something different on the Day of Resurrection. In the Quran, God reflects on this: "He asks: 'When is the Day of Resurrection?' When vision is dazzled, and the Moon is eclipsed, and the Sun and the Moon are joined together. On that Day, man will say: 'Where is the escape?'" (75:6–10).

Let us appreciate God's creation of the Moon, which is very apparent to anyone camping at night. The Moon gives us so much light in the darkness of the night, despite the fact that it has no brightness of its own, but all its light is a reflection of the Sun's brightness. In the Quran (10:5), God says: "It is He who made the Sun radiant, and the Moon a light."

The Sun and Moon allow us to divide time into days and nights. "And of His signs are the night and the day, and the Sun and the Moon" (41:37).

The Sun and Moon allow us to divide time into months and years, using either a solar or lunar calendar.

All of this was apparent to the early Muslims, as it is to us today. In the Quran, God reminds us that all this is a mercy from Him, and a sign of His existence. "Then which of your Lord's marvels will you deny?" (55:13). This is so important that he repeats it 31 times in this chapter, Surat ar-Rahman "The Compassionate".

17 Stars

Another of the signs of God (Allah) that are easily visible to us, as they were to the early Muslims, is stars. The most obvious star is the Sun, which provides light and heat, and is thus essential for life on Earth.

However, the account below is of the stars that are visible while camping at night.

It was a cold night. Freezing! After all, we were in the South Island of New Zealand in winter. So what would you expect? As we were gazing upwards, the sky glittered with an abundance of stars. This was Tekapo.

A Dark-Sky Reserve

The Aoraki Mackenzie International Dark-Sky Reserve is well known for the prominence and clarity of its night sky. This is a dark sky location, where light pollution from artificial sources such as housing and street lights is minimal. As a result, the darkness of the night sky, and the brightness of the stars in it, can be seen clearly. This makes it an ideal location for scientific observation.

> An IDA [International Dark-Sky Association] International Dark-Sky Reserve is a public or private land possessing an exceptional or distinguished quality of starry nights and nocturnal environment that is specifically protected for its scientific, natural, educational, cultural, heritage and/or public enjoyment.[1]

When this article was originally written in 2017, Tekapo was one of only 11 such sites in the world, the others being:

- Brecon Beacons National Park (Wales)
- Exmoor National Park (England)
- Kerry (Ireland)
- Mont-Mégantic (Canada)
- Moore's Reserve (England)
- NamibRand Nature Reserve (Namibia)
- Pic du Midi (France)
- Rhön (Germany)
- Snowdonia National Park (Wales)
- Westhavelland (Germany)

Since then, ten more sites have been added[1].

It is a one-of-a-kind wonder. While in Tekapo, we gazed at the beauty of the night sky. We saw what looked like a million stars, glittering in the night sky. A very special moment indeed.

We made our way to our stargazing tour. As we gazed at the night sky, the Milky Way, the galaxy with its billions of stars, was so clear and visible. The tour guide talked us through the stars we were seeing. Through a telescope, we saw Saturn – technically a planet, not a star – with its beautiful rings.

"By the sky and at-Tariq. But what will let you know what at-Tariq is? The Piercing Star. There is no soul without a Protector over it" (86:1-4). Some commentators say that "the piercing star" refers to Saturn.

Stars as metaphors

Regardless of whether we look up at the night sky or not, the stars are suspended high above by the will of the Almighty. Just as the stars watch over us at night, God is letting us know that for every soul there is a protector. We may forget this fact when we go about our daily lives. The stars are a sign of this.

"By the star when it sets" (53:1). Scholars say this verse refers to the Pleiades, or Seven Sisters. When the star sets, everything becomes so clear with the approach of the dawn. God swears by this as it is something that we as humans can perceive as stable in the universe. In another place, God says: "I swear by the locations of the stars. It is an oath, if you only knew, that is tremendous. It is a noble Quran in a well-protected Book" (56:75-78). Again, God is focusing on the truth of this book. The noble Quran that he has granted us is a blessing to find the way to Him.

The stars are also a blessing from God, in that they allow humans to navigate, especially sailors at sea, where there are no landmarks. This was done in the time of Prophet Muhammad (pbuh) by observation of the position of the Sun and other stars, aided in later years by instruments such as the astrolabe and sextant. Nowadays, satellite-aided GPS has replaced this. In the Quran, God reminds us of the navigation afforded by the stars: "And it is He Who created the stars for you, that you may be guided by them in the darkness of land and sea. We thus explain the revelations for people who know" (6:97).

Back in Tekapo, I was thrilled to count as many as ten shooting stars within a couple of hours. Watching them shoot in every direction was amazing. This reminds us of a verse in the Quran that talks about something similar: "When the stars are dimmed" (81:2). That is, all the planets and stars will scatter in the universe, as a sign of the Day of Judgement. It is not so farfetched to imagine this when we look upon the sky and see shooting stars. This is also something that we will need to face for sure. There is no doubt about it.

As we travel and see the signs of our Lord and their beauty, let us remind ourselves: "So which of your Lord's marvels will you deny?" (55:13).

1 International Dark-Sky Association (n.d.). *International dark sky reserves.* https://www.darksky.org/idsp/reserves/

18 Mountains

Living in New Zealand, one of the best ways to see the beauty that God (Allah) has created is to travel the country. The South Island displays this beauty magnificently, although the North Island has its share as well. A major factor in this is the country's mountains. Being situated on the join of two of the Earth's tectonic plates, the country has many mountains. It is no wonder that it was chosen as the setting for the Lord of the Rings and Hobbit films.

What is it about the beautiful view of a mountain that attracts mankind so much, whether in summer, with trees in lush green, or in winter, with the snow-capped mountains painted in white? They stand tall, as indicators of New Zealand's volcanic past.

"And at the mountains – how they are installed." (88:19)

"And he cast mountains on the Earth, lest it shifts with you." (16:15)

The reason mountains are firmly fixed is a feature that the early Muslims would have been totally unaware of. As tectonic plates meet, not only does one part rise up, forming mountains, but also the other part descends further into the Earth. In the Quran, God explains: "And the mountains [as] pegs" (78:7). These pegs are like tent pegs, used to make sure a tent is firmly fixed and will not blow away.

The deafening silence

We are struck in awe at the majestic beauty of the mountains. We go out of our way to book a cruise around Milford Sound and Doubtful Sound to have a breathtaking view of them. When we go up close, we feel we are connected with nature.

As we took a cruise around Doubtful Sound, at one point the captain of the boat stopped the engine and asked us to have a moment of silence. He asked us to stand or sit still, with no clicking of cameras, and no movement on board. In complete silence, we took in the magnificent beauty of the surrounding waterfalls, mountains, sky, water, and the sound of the wind blowing, birds chirping, the water splashing. The experience in itself cannot be taken in photographs or videos. One has to be there to feel it.

Mountains as homes

God talks about the mountains at the time of the Thamud tribe: “They used to carve homes in the mountains, feeling secure” (15:82).

The mountains give us a feeling of stability. God says in another verse in the Quran, where the bees are also given refuge in the mountains: “And your Lord inspired the bee: ‘Set up hives in the mountains, and in the trees, and in what they construct’” (16:68).

Even mountains will disappear

The beauty of the mountains is only temporary. Just as mountains have risen and fallen over millions of years, so today’s mountains that seem so sturdy will eventually fall. In the Quran, God talks of the majesty of the mountains and what will happen to them: “On the Day when the Earth and the mountains tremble, and the mountains become heaps of sand” (73:14).

This magnificent beauty of which we are in awe, will one day be a mirage: “And the mountains are removed and will be [but] a mirage” (78:20).

Just like the end of life of mankind, the mountains themselves will also be turned to dust.

“And the mountains are set in motion, and become a mirage” (81:3).

“And the mountains are crushed and crumble” (56:5).

“And the mountains are blown away” (77:10).

“And the mountains will be like tufted wool” (70:9 and 101:5).

As we travel, let us appreciate the signs that God has provided us. Let us recognize them as signs of God’s magnificence and ponder on them. However, we also need to acknowledge that this too will one day come to a close.

“So which of the marvels of your Lord will you deny?” (55:13).

19 Climbing into the sky

Deaths on Everest

The first person to climb the world's highest mountain, Mount Everest, was New Zealander Sir Edmund Hillary, with Sherpa Tenzing Norgay, in 1953. Since then, the feat of conquering Everest has always been the pinnacle of mountaineering achievement.

However, the ascent of Everest is a very dangerous enterprise, and over the last two decades, on average about six people per year have lost their lives trying to reach the summit.

In 2019, an alarming photo[1] showed a human traffic jam at the summit. Four reasons were suggested why the death toll has been so high.

Firstly, Cyclone Fani hit India and Bangladesh on 5 May 2019 and as a result, a few days later, the weather in the Himalayas deteriorated. The Nepalese government suspended all mountaineering activities for more than two days. The routine of attaching bolted ropes to help climbers was also delayed. When they were fixed, the first fair-weather window was 19 – 20 May. However, most teams decided to wait until the second window on 22 – 24 May. This delay led to various logistical problems.

Secondly, on 23 May a total of more than 250 climbers attempted to reach the summit, the largest daily number ever. This caused congestion near the summit, and some climbers had to wait for hours, both on their ascent and their descent. There were thus two rows of climbers, one ascending and one descending; they both have to use the same ropes. At that altitude, climbers use oxygen cylinders, and the delay made their oxygen run low.

Thirdly, it has been reported that there has been a rise in the number of relatively inexperienced climbers on Everest. As the world's highest mountain, Everest is an unforgiving environment, and weather conditions can turn dangerous quickly. Most climbers are accompanied by Sherpas, who are native Nepalese and thus used to high altitudes, and are elite mountaineers. However, if the weather turns bad, the Sherpas have to take care of themselves. It has long been suggested that the Nepalese government should introduce qualifying criteria for people applying for permits to climb Everest, such as that they must have climbed mountains over 6,000 m (6 km).

Finally, as the number of people wanting to climb Everest has increased, so has the number of operators. Newer operators try to break into the market by offering cheaper prices, which then forces more established operators to reduce their prices, and hire cheaper, less experienced guides. While the price of the government permits is fixed at US$11,000, the prices of the operators follow market forces.

Covid affected the number of people permitted to attempt the Everest climb in 2020 and 2021. The annual record, set in 2019, was 807 successful climbers, and numbers have since recovered to the same pre-Covid level.

Altitude sickness

A major problem for anyone climbing high mountains is the amount of oxygen in the air. Because of its energy content, oxygen is vital for humans and other living beings. At sea level, air contains about 21% oxygen. However, at higher altitudes, the percentage of oxygen in the air decreases. At about 5,500 m (5.5 km), the concentration of oxygen is about half that at sea level. And at the summit of Mount Everest, oxygen levels are about 30% those at sea level. As a result, in order to maintain a similar oxygen intake into the blood, the lungs and heart have to work harder, by breathing faster and beating faster. Even by breathing and beating faster, the body still cannot reach the same oxygen intake levels as at sea level.

This may lead to altitude sickness. This sickness starts to occur in some people at altitudes above about 2,500 m (2.5 km). This even leads to problems for some skiers, because many ski resorts are situated at altitudes of 2,500 m.

Altitude sickness does not affect everyone. It typically affects about 20% of people ascending to 2,500 m, and 40% of those going to 3,000 m (3 km). Mount Everest is three times higher than this, at 8,848 m (nearly 9 km).

A person's susceptibility to altitude sickness depends on many factors:

- the faster you climb
- if you normally live at or near sea level
- if you have had altitude sickness before
- if you have not acclimatized to the altitude
- consuming alcohol and other substances
- if you have medical problems relating to the heart, nervous system, or lungs
- your age, weight and general fitness

There are various symptoms of altitude sickness:

- breathlessness
- headaches
- dizziness
- pins and needles
- swelling of the hands, feet and face
- vomiting
- tiredness
- difficulty sleeping
- loss of appetite

While altitude sickness is a debilitating problem, there is fortunately a relatively simple remedy: descend to a lower altitude, where there will be a greater concentration of oxygen in the air.

Altitude sickness in the Quran

How does this relate to Islam? In the Quran (6:125), God (Allah) states:

> Whomever God desires to guide, He spreads open his heart to Islam; and whomever He desires to misguide, He makes his heart narrow, constricted, as though he were climbing up the sky. God thus lays defilement upon those who do not believe.

In *tafsir* explanation of this verse, commentators have tended to concentrate on the meaning of "expanding and constricting the breast", interpreting it as a metaphor for believers accepting and disbelievers rejecting faith in the heart.

"This is a parable that Allah has given for the heart of the disbeliever, which is completely impassable and closed to faith" (Abu Jafar bin Jarir).

As for the second part ("as though he were climbing up the sky"), commentators have interpreted this as a metaphor for something that is impossible.

"The example of his inability to climb up to the sky, which is beyond his capability and power" (Abu Jafar bin Jarir).

"As though he were engaged in something impossible" (Kashani).

However, as the Everest episode illustrates, there is another possible interpretation that is simpler and more literal. People who are climbing Mount Everest, or other high mountains, are climbing into the sky, i.e. to a high altitude. The explanation of altitude sickness in *Medical News Today*[2] uses phraseology that is almost identical to "constricting the breast" in the Quran: "Chest tightness is an indicator that symptoms of altitude sickness are becoming complicated."

It is also worth noting that there are no very high mountains in the Arabian Peninsula. There are some that are around 3,000 m, including Jabal Sawda, Jabal Ferwa, Jabal Natfa, Jabal Warrab, Jabal Al-Majaz and Jabal As-Seqaa. They are all in the Sarawat Mountains which run parallel to the western coast of the Arabian Peninsula. They are only about a third the height of Mount Everest. The problem of altitude sickness may therefore not be apparent to commentators from this region.

Various commentators on the Quran have listed scientific statements in the text that could not have been known to people in the time of Prophet Muhammad (pbuh) and the early Muslims, but which have been shown to be accurate by later, often very recent, scientific discoveries. The fact that the chest becomes tighter, and breathing more difficult, when climbing to high altitudes, may be another such scientific revelation.

1 Khadka, N. S. (2019). Everest deaths: Four reasons why this climbing season went wrong. *BBC News*, 28 May 2019. https://www.bbc.com/news/world-asia-48423738

2 Medical News Today (2021). *Altitude sickness: Causes, symptoms, and treatment.* https://www.medicalnewstoday.com/articles/179819.php

3

The Quran

The Quran

In Section 1, we saw that belief in God is a very central aspect of Islam. Indeed, it is one half of the declaration of faith (*shahadah*) that defines a Muslim. Among the other articles of belief in Islam are that God has revealed scripture to messengers, the last of whom was Prophet Muhammad (pbuh).

Muslims thus believe that the Quran is the verbatim (word-for-word) word of God revealed over a period of 23 years via Angel Gabriel (Jibril). Section 2, on the signs of Allah, included some descriptions in the Quran of physical phenomena that could not have been known to people in Muhammad's time. They are thus persuasive evidence that the Quran was indeed written by God.

This section starts by asking the reverse question: "How do we know that Muhammad did not write the Quran?" The signs of Allah in Section 2 argue that Muhammad could not have known the truth of parts of the Quran. The first chapter in this section gives nine more arguments that the Quran is the verbatim word of God, and was not written by Muhammad.

Critical literacy is an approach based on the fact that writing is seldom neutral, but is influenced by the writer's biases and agenda. Not accepting everything at face value has become increasingly important in the modern world of the internet, social media, and pervasive misinformation. The second chapter explains seven questions that should be asked about any piece of writing, including the Quran.

Finally, there are many people in the world, probably millions, who have memorized the whole of the Quran in its original Arabic (they are *hafith*). What better way to know and follow the teachings of the Quran than to have memorized it?

20 Did Muhammad write the Quran?

If you ask a Muslim what his miracle is, he will go over and take his miracle off the bookshelf and hand it to you, and you can read it: it is the Quran. It is a miracle that we can all touch and read and experience.

If this tangible book is the miracle, then the next question to ask is where it came from and who wrote it. Many non-Muslims reply that it was written by Prophet Muhammad (pbuh), because they do not want to admit that it might be the word of God (Allah). This accusation is not a new one; it originated before the death of Muhammad, and so is 14 centuries old. God mentions it in the Quran itself: "Or do they say: 'He [Muhammad] made this Quran up!'" (46:8) However, the accusation seems to be brought up more in our time as attacks on Muhammad and the religion seem to get more frequent. It is popular nowadays for people to discard the Quran as just man-made and accuse Muhammad of writing the Quran himself.

This chapter examines nine criteria that argue for the fact that Muhammad did not write the Quran.

1. Illiteracy

Firstly, Muhammad was illiterate. He could not read or write, and is often referred to as the "unlettered prophet". In the story of the very first revelation, which took place in the cave on Jabal An-Nur on the outskirts of Makkah, Jibril said to Muhammad: "Iqra" ("Read"). Muhammad replied: "I cannot read."

The Quran itself reminds us that Muhammad was illiterate:

> "Those who follow the Messenger, the Unlettered Prophet, ..." (7:157)

> "You O Prophet could not read any writing even before this revelation, nor could you write at all. Otherwise, the people of falsehood would have been suspicious" (29:48).

In short, Muhammad was illiterate, and could not write.

2 .The message and the messenger

In various places, the Quran states that it is a revelation from God, not from Muhammad, e.g.: "The revelation of the Book is from God, the Exalted in Might, the Wise" (45:2).

In other places, it also states that Muhammad is just a messenger, a human being, e.g.: "We sent you only universally to all people, a herald and warner, but most people do not know" (34:28).

The verse quoted above continues: "Those who follow the Messenger, the Unlettered Prophet, whom they find mentioned in the Torah and the Gospel in their possession, ..." (7:157).

This relates to a passage in the Bible: "The Lord your God will raise up for you a prophet like me [Moses] from among you, from your brothers – it is to him you shall listen" (Deuteronomy 18:15). Muhammad – and not Jesus – is like Moses in that both had normal human births, both had human parents, both married, both were accepted by their people, both brought new laws, and both were buried on this Earth. Neither Muhammad nor Moses claimed to be God, neither is said to have died for our sins, and neither had an other-worldly kingdom.

So, even the Bible describes Muhammad as a prophet with a message.

3. Language

Muslims have a record of Muhammad's teaching in the Sunnah, the record of how he implemented Islam in daily life – what he said, what he did, and what others did that he did not disapprove of. Many of Muhammad's actions and exact words are preserved in the hadith literature, which runs to several large volumes.

There are thus two authoritative sources in Islam: the Quran, which Muslims believe to be the verbatim word of God, and the hadiths, which are the reported teachings of Muhammad. The language of both books is Arabic, but the form of the language differs greatly between them.

The hadiths are in the normal oral usage of Muhammad. Those who heard him speak acknowledged his words as concise, forceful, and persuasive, as is befitting someone contemplating God with appropriate gravity. But they were still the words of a 7th century CE Arab.

In contrast, when people heard and memorized the Quran, they recognized that it had a transcendent majesty and substance that was not the words of a 7th century CE Arab. They were overcome by rapture and reverence.

This difference in language may be difficult for non-native speakers of Arabic to appreciate. However, native Arabic speakers often shed tears when reciting the Quran, but typically do not when quoting hadiths.

4. A challenge

The Quran challenges its readers, especially those who disbelieve in it, to prove that it is not from God. The first people to claim it was written by Muhammad were the Prophet's own opponents, as we read in the Quran: "When Our revelations are recited to them, plain and clear, those who disbelieve say of the truth when it has come to them: 'This is obviously magic.' Or do they say: 'He invented it himself?'" (46:7–8).

They were desperate to protect their interests against the rising tide of Islam and hoped, as do their modern counterparts, to spread doubt about the Quran's divine authorship, so that Muslims would start doubting its authority as well.

The Quran also states that it is an incomparable work: "Say: 'If mankind and *jinn* [invisible beings] came together to produce the like of this Quran, they could never produce the like of it, even if they backed up one another'" (17:88).

If Muhammad had written the Quran, surely he would not have inserted these challenges to the reader. And if he, as a mortal human being, had written it, then these challenges would be easy to complete.

5. Self-criticism

If Muhammad had written the Quran, it would be strange for him to include a passage criticizing himself. This is exactly what Surat Abasa (80) gives us:

> He frowned and turned away when the blind man approached him. But how do you know? Perhaps he was seeking to purify himself, or be reminded, and the message would benefit him. But as for him who was indifferent, you gave him your attention, though you are not liable if he does not purify himself. But as for him who came to you seeking, in awe, to him you were inattentive. Do not. This is a Lesson. Whoever wills, shall remember it (80: 1-12).

The Clear Quran[1], in its commentary on this chapter, describes the episode that this revelation relates to:

> In a hadith collected by At-Tirmizi, a blind man by the name of Abdullah ibn Umm Maktum, an early Muslim, came to the Prophet seeking to learn more about the faith, while the Prophet was in the middle of a discussion with an elite Makkan pagan, trying to convince him to abandon his idols and believe in the One True God. Abdullah was so impatient that he interrupted the discussion several times. The Prophet frowned and turned all his attention to the man he was already talking to. This Makkan surah was later revealed, telling the Prophet that he should have tended to the faithful man who was eager to learn. After this surah was revealed, the Prophet would honour Abdullah, calling him "the man for whom my Lord rebuked me".

If Muhammad had written the Quran, would he really include self-criticism?

6. Signs

If Muhammad had written the Quran, it could not include information that Arabs of his time would have no understanding of, and that have only been explained by science in the last few decades and centuries. Examples of this have been given in Section 2 on the signs of God.

7. Predictions

If Muhammad wrote the Quran, it could contain predictions that might or might not come true. However, if God wrote the Quran, any such predictions would have to be accurate.

In the Quran (48:27), God states that the Muslims in Madinah, after the Hijrah migration, would return to Makkah in safety: "You will enter the Sacred Mosque [in Makkah], God willing, in security, heads shaven, or hair cut short, not fearing. He knew what you did not know, and has granted besides that an imminent victory." This came about in 630 CE.

The above chapter continues (48:28): "It is He who sent His Messenger with the guidance and the religion of truth, to make it prevail over all religions." Islam quickly spread throughout the Middle East. It is predicted to be the world's largest religion by population by the end of the 21st century CE (see Chapter 46).

The Persian Empire defeated the Roman Empire in Syria (613 CE) and Jerusalem (615 CE). However, the Quran (30:2-4) predicted that the Romans would eventually prevail. "The Romans have been defeated in a nearby territory. But following their defeat, they will be victorious in a few years." The Roman (Byzantine) emperor Heraclius defeated the Persians in a series of battles starting with Issus in Anatolia (eastern Türkiye) in 622 CE, and ending with Nineveh in 627 CE.

8. The Quran and the Bible

The Quran contains some of the same stories as in the Bible. Muslims see no problem in this, in that the Quran is the word of God, and God is the original source of material that is in the Bible.

The Bible is in Hebrew (Old Testament) and Greek (New Testament). Muhammad spoke neither of these languages, and there was no Arabic translation of the Bible in his time. So, even if Muhammad were not illiterate, he could not read the Bible and learn these stories.

Even if he did know some of these stories, the fact is that the stories in the Quran are sometimes different from those in the Bible. The story of Adam is one such example. In the Bible, he and Eve (Hawwa) commit what is known in Christianity as "original sin", condemning mankind to being born sinful and needing to be saved through Jesus (Isa). In contrast, in the Quran, Adam and Eve realize their wrongs and repent, and are forgiven by God, e.g. (7:23): "They said: 'Our Lord, we have done wrong to ourselves. Unless You forgive us, and have mercy on us, we will be among the losers.'"

9. Characters in the Quran

Muhammad was an Arab, and the Arabs and Jews are noted for their rivalry. However, the name of Jesus, a Jew, is mentioned 25 times in the Quran, more than the name of Muhammad. If Muhammad had written the Quran, surely he would have inserted his name more often than that of Jesus.

Mary (Mariam) the mother of Jesus (and therefore also Jewish) has a whole chapter named after her (#19). Not only this but the grandfather of Jesus, Joachim (Imran), also has a chapter named after him and his family (Surat Ali Imran "The family of Imran", #3).

If Muhammad had written the Quran, surely he would have inserted the names of members of his family. However, there is no mention of any of them; there is no Surat Aminah (his mother), no Surat Abdullah (his father), no Surah Khadijah or Aisha (wives), no Surah Hamzah (his uncle), and so on.

In conclusion, there are many arguments that show that Muhammad did not write the Quran. He did not have any schooling that covered the knowledge described in the Quran, such as knowledge of historical events, previous prophets and natural phenomena. Also, the language of the Quran is very different from that of the hadith, the everyday sayings of Muhammad. Finally, it is well known that Muhammad was illiterate and it therefore is impossible that he could have composed such a monumental work.

1 Mustafa Khattab (2016). *The clear Quran with Arabic text: A thematic English translation of the message of the final revelation.* Furqaan Institute of Quranic Education.

21 Critical literacy and the Quran

Do you believe everything you see in writing? Hopefully not, because many writers have their own "agendas", that is, they are writing from a particular point of view that you may or may not agree with. In other words, it is always wise to adopt a critical and questioning approach to what you read, and not accept everything at face value, because most writing is not neutral in this sense.

This is the basis of a popular approach to literacy instruction and general English language teaching in some countries. It is known as critical literacy. The website ReadWriteThink[1] gives a concise definition: "Critical literacy involves reading critically – thinking about the identity and intent of the writer, and the social and historical context in which the text was written."

The word *critical* in *critical literacy* does not imply criticism, that is, a negative approach to a piece of writing. Instead, it is like critiquing, implying a detailed and analytical questioning approach.

Let us carry out a brief critical literacy analysis of the Quran, by asking several pertinent questions.

1. Is the Quran a book? Does it refer to itself as a book?

The Quran is plainly a book, in the limited sense that it is printed pages between covers. However, we need to ask whether it is a book in the sense of a coherent work in terms of content.

The Quran refers to itself in several places as a book: "These are the Verses of the Clear Book" (12:1).

So the Quran refers to itself and calls itself a book. It also calls itself the "Quran" ("recitation"): "… and chant the Quran rhythmically" (73:4).

2. In what language was the Quran written or revealed?

The Quran is in Arabic. Any translation of the Quran into another language is simply that – a translation. In several places in the Quran itself, God (Allah) makes this point. The extract quoted above continues: "These are the Verses of the Clear Book. We have revealed it an Arabic Quran, so that you may understand" (12:1-2).

As noted in chapter 3, the Quran (41:44) also points out the simple logic that Arabic is the language of the Quran because Prophet Muhammad (pbuh), to whom it was revealed, was an Arab and spoke Arabic. That is, it is nonsense to reveal a non-Arabic Quran to an Arabic speaker.

Many commentators have rightly argued that you cannot translate the Quran into English or any other language without losing some of its original nuances of meaning and imagery. For this reason, many translations of the Quran are not entitled *The Quran*, but rather *The Meaning of the Quran* or some such phrase.

3. Who wrote the Quran? Does the Quran claim to be from God?

Muslims believe the Quran is verbatim (word-for-word) the word of God. And the Quran itself confirms this in many places, by claiming to be from God: "The revelation of the Book, without a doubt, is from the Lord of the Universe" (32:2).

4. Does the Quran contain information that only God would know?

If the Quran was written by God, this would be proved by including in the Quran evidence and statements that only God would know to be true. Such evidence is examined in Section 2, which presents scientific facts that are far beyond the rudimentary understanding of people in Muhammad's time, and that have been proven by modern scientists to be true only in the last century or two.

The early Muslims would not have understood these scientific statements in the Quran but, believing it to be the word of God, they did not think to change anything. And many centuries later, science has shown them to be accurate.

5. When and where was the Quran written or revealed?

The chronologically first revelation of the Quran (96:1-5) was delivered to Muhammad by Angel Gabriel (Jibril) in the year 610 CE: "Read: In the Name of your Lord who created …". The final revelation came in 632, shortly before Muhammad's death: "Today I have perfected your religion for you, ..." (5:3) This was a period of 22 years.

The Makkan phase of the revelation lasted about 13 years, from the first revelation (in the cave Hira on the outskirts of Makkah) up to the Hijrah (migration to Madinah). This phase is determined by the prime task of Muhammad to call people to Islam. The main themes of this call, based on the Quranic revelation, are:

- God and His unity (*tauhid*)
- The coming resurrection and judgement
- Righteous conduct

The Madinan phase lasted about ten years, from the Hijrah to the death of Muhammad. While the three themes from the Makkan phase continue, the fact that the Muslims had established a community (ummah) produces a greater emphasis on more everyday matters. The topics of these Madinan verses often deal with practical matters such as the treatment of women and orphans, and inheritance.

The historical episode leading to certain revelations is known. In the previous chapter, Surat Abasa ("He frowned") was quoted, in order to argue that Muhammad would not criticize himself. The context and the background necessary for understanding the text are known. Who frowned? Why did he frown?

Another example is Surat at-Tahrim ("The Prohibition" #66). Although it is a short 12-verse chapter, it is almost impossible to understand from the text, without a description of the context in which it was revealed, namely jealousy between the wives he married after his first wife of 25 years, Khadijah, passed away. *The Clear Quran*[2] supplies this in a clarifying introduction:

> This Madinan surah deals with an incident that happened within the Prophet's household. The Prophet used to visit all of his wives in the evening. It so happened that he stayed longer than usual at the house of Zainab bint Jahsh, where he was offered honey – something he liked very much. Out of jealousy, two other wives (Hafsah and Aishah) agreed between themselves to tell the Prophet, when he visited each of them, that his mouth gave off a bad smell, knowing that he did not like bad smells. Eventually, the Prophet made an

oath that he would never eat honey again, and told Hafsah not to tell anyone about this. But she told Aishah that their plan worked. Both wives are subtly advised to learn from the example of the two believing women mentioned at the end of the surah – Mary and Asiyah, the wife of Pharoah – and take a lesson from the fate of the wives of Noah and Lot, who were both destroyed despite being wives of prophets.

The names of the wives are not mentioned in the chapter, nor is honey, or other details, even though we know the incident that triggered the revelation. The point of the chapter is to warn against jealousy, and against telling lies, gossip and backbiting, and to remind everyone of the possible consequences.

6. Who is the Quran for? Who are the intended readership?

In various places in the Quran, it is explicitly stated who is being addressed:

- Believers, e.g. "O you who believe! Repent to God with sincere repentance" (66:8).
- Disbelievers, e.g. "Say, 'O disbelievers. I do not worship what you worship'" (109:1-2).
- Mankind, e.g. "O people! We created you from a male and a female …" (49:13).

The Quran is indeed intended for everyone: "It is only a Reminder to all mankind" (81:27).

7. What is the purpose of the Quran?

This is perhaps the most important question to be asked in critical literacy. Why did the author write this? What was he/she trying to achieve by writing it? What effect did the writer hope to have on the readers, after they read it? In various places, the Quran describes itself as a book of wisdom, that clarifies things, as good news and warning, teaching, a guide and a mercy.

"We revealed to you the Scripture only to clarify for them what they differ about, and guidance and mercy for people who believe" (16:64).

"These are the Signs of the Quran, a book that makes things clear. Guidance and good news for the believers" (27:1-2).

The questions asked above are all simple questions. They are mostly the *wh*-questions: *who, why, when, where, how?* And for the Quran we have simple answers, with historical or internal evidence. The Quran is the revealed word of God (*who*) and contains information that only He would have known at the time of revelation. It was written for mankind (*who*). It was written as a book of wisdom, a guide, a mercy, etc. (*why*). It was revealed by Gabriel (Jibril) (*how*) in Makkah and Madinah (*where*) between 610 and 632 CE (*when*). It is in Arabic (*how*). The Quran refers to itself as a book, and as the Quran ("recitation").

Readers might like to ask the same questions about other scriptures that they are familiar with.

1 ReadWriteThink (n.d.). *Critical literacy.* https://www.readwritethink.org/files/resources/lesson_images/lesson1009/critical.pdf

2 Mustafa Khattab (2016). *The clear Quran with Arabic text: A thematic English translation of the message of the final revelation.* Furqaan Institute of Quranic Education.

22 The importance of memorization

Fahrenheit 451

Fahrenheit 451 is a 1953 novel by the US science-fiction writer Ray Bradbury. It has twice been made into a film, in 1966 and 2018. It is a dystopian novel, meaning one describing a fictional future state which is the opposite of utopia. It is a future American society in which the masses are pleasure-seeking and anti-intellectual. Reading books is banned, as it may lead to critical thought. The central character, Guy Montag, is employed as a "fireman". However, in this dystopian future, "fireman" means "book-burner". The purpose of the fire service is not to put out fires; it is to start them in order to burn books. The punishment for reading books, or for having them in your house, is to be sent to a mental hospital. The books are burned "for the good of humanity".

This central element of the plot of Bradbury's book was inspired by the book-burning of Nazis in 1933. Books that did not conform with Nazi ideology were destroyed. It had a precedent in 18th century CE Germany. Germany was, at that time, a collection of individual states. Those people demonstrating for a unified Germany – especially students – burned books which they considered anti-national or anti-German.

The novel's title *Fahrenheit 451* refers to the supposed temperature at which book paper spontaneously combusts, although in fact the temperature is around 450°C, much higher.

Drugs are administered to the people, and they are fed information by huge television screens. In this way, the government ensures the people fall in line with its policies.

One day, while the fire service are searching the house of an old lady, before finding books and then burning them, Montag glances at some pages of a book and, on a whim, steals it. Over the next year, he steals dozens of books and hides them in his own house. He reads them and tries to memorize them in order to preserve their contents, before the physical books are burned.

He enlists the help of Faber, a former English teacher, and from him learns the way books attempt to describe and explain human existence.

The fire chief eventually learns that Montag has been hiding books, and leads a crew to Montag's house, where they find the books, and burn the house down. As a result, Montag starts to question the government policy of book-burning. Having been exposed as a book-hoarder, he has the choice of returning to his job or fleeing.

Knowing the consequences of being caught, he escapes to the countryside, where Faber lives. There, he meets like-minded people who spend all day memorizing and reciting books, so that they are preserved and it does not matter if the printed copies are burned.

Yesterday

Yesterday is the title of a 2019 film, written by Richard Curtis, and based on a story by Jack Barth. The plot revolves around the character of British Indian Jack Malik, who is a struggling singer-songwriter. He is about to give up singing in clubs, but his manager and childhood friend Ellie tries to persuade him to persevere.

One night, after a freak cycle accident with a bus during a mysterious global blackout, he finds that he is the only person who knows who the Beatles were. It is as if the Beatles and all their music had never existed.

This is of course music to Jack's ears. Jack racks his brain to try to remember all the songs on all the Beatles albums, and their lyrics. His first source for research is, of course, Google. However, in this alternative world, a search for "Beatles" only finds the insects – beetles. He googles for the title of their 1967 record *Sergeant Pepper*, but only finds capsicum peppers. He is seen trying desperately to piece together the dense lyrics of the Beatles classic *Eleanor Rigby*. He frantically tries to remember whether it is Eleanor or Father McKenzie who was darning socks.

Nevertheless, he reconstructs enough of the Beatles' catalogue to become a smash hit overnight playing their songs to audiences who have never heard them before.

Eventually he meets two elderly Beatles fans who say that they know that the Beatles – not Jack – wrote all the songs. Nevertheless, they are happy that Jack is keeping the songs alive, albeit in a stripped-down voice-and-guitar version.

Ultimately, Jack decides that he needs to tell the truth, and confesses, during a performance at Wembley Stadium, that he did not write the songs.

The fact that Jack can reconstruct most of the Beatles' songs shows their popularity. John Lennon of the Beatles claimed in a 1966 newspaper interview that the Beatles were more popular than Jesus. His exact words are often misquoted:

> Christianity will go. It will vanish and shrink. I needn't argue about that; I'm right and I'll be proved right. We're more popular than Jesus now; I don't know which will go first – rock 'n' roll or Christianity. Jesus was all right but his disciples were thick and ordinary. It's them twisting it that ruins it for me.

This prompted a backlash in the USA – but not in the UK – where Christians protested by burning copies of the Beatles' records. It is debatable whether the statement – that the Beatles were more popular than Jesus – was true in 1966. According to one source[1], the world population in 1966 was 3.4 billion, with 1.2 billion Christians. However, what Lennon and everyone else overlooked was that Jesus is and was a revered prophet of God in Islam, with 577 million Muslims in 1966.

Memorizing the classics

It is appealing to speculate how much of the classics of the arts could be reconstructed if all physical archives – written, painted or recorded documentation of them – were lost. This is essentially what a lot of science fiction is about – asking the question: "What if?"

Many plays could probably be reconstructed, if all copies were burned, from the memory of actors who had appeared on stage in those plays (although any one actor may not have memorized all the parts of any play).

Similarly, people often memorize favorite poems, and give recitals of these, and those poems could perhaps be reconstructed from people's memories.

Musicians like Jack Malik regularly play songs and, as in *Yesterday*, could reproduce many of them. Similarly, orchestral conductors, players and opera singers could reconstruct classical music.

Art students are often taught by being made to reproduce works of art in galleries, as part of their instruction.

Less likely to be reconstructed are whole books, as they are not performed. People often like to memorize favorite extracts from books, in the same way that they memorize poetry. However, it is rare for anyone to memorize a whole book.

Memorizing the Quran

The Quran is the one book where we could be certain that there are enough people in the world today who know it by heart in order to be able to reconstruct a written version of it.

The Quran was revealed to Prophet Muhammad (pbuh) by the Angel Gabriel (Jibril) in pieces over a period of 23 years. Muhammad lived in 7th century CE Arabia in a time when many people were not literate, and indeed Muhammad himself could not read or write.

The Quran was preserved in two ways. First, the Arabs preserved their histories, genealogies, and poetry by memory alone. Muhammad would memorize the verses as they were revealed. In this sense, we can say that Muhammad was the very first *hafith* (person who has memorized the whole Quran). When Muhammad repeated the verses of the Quran, his followers naturally preserved the words by memorizing them, and thus his followers were the earliest hafiths. Memorization required no expensive raw materials (in an age when there was no paper in the Muslim world). Memorization was also considered more secure – a manuscript could easily be destroyed (as in the science fiction of *Fahrenheit 451*), but if the Quran was to be memorized by many hafiths, it would never be lost.

The Arabic word *hafith* means both "memorizer" and also "guardian", a reference to the fact that the original Quran is being guarded by being memorized by so many people. In the Quran, God (Allah) states that the Quran will not be corrupted: "Surely We revealed the Message, and We will surely preserve it" (15:9).

"Those who reject the Reminder when it has come to them—it is an invincible Book. Falsehood cannot approach it, from before it or behind it. It is a revelation from One Wise and Praiseworthy" (41:41-2).

Second, the Quran was preserved through writing. Whenever any revelation took place, it was written down at once on tablets, palm branches, or animal skin, primarily by Zaid bin Thabit, who was the main scribe out of the 42 scribes of the revelation. Muhammad set the order of the chapters under the guidance of Gabriel and ordered his companions to maintain that order. Abu Bakr, the first caliph of Islam, compiled the Quran, and Uthman, the third caliph, made numerous copies and sent one copy to each state capital. Two of these original copies still exist: one in the Topkapi Museum, Istanbul, Türkiye, and the other in Tashkent, Uzbekistan. Even after Uthman collected and organized a written version of the Quran, recitation (from memory) of the Quran was still honored and encouraged.

Hafiths

Hafiths are highly respected within the Islamic community, and are tested on their knowledge. For example, in one test they are asked to continue the recitation of a passage taken randomly from the Quran. As they do not know which passage will be chosen, they must know the whole text in order to be sure of passing. In another test, a would-be hafith might be asked to recite verses containing a specific word or phrase. Most hafiths have studied as children in Islamic schools (*madrasahs*), being instructed in *tajwid* (rules of recitation) and vocalization as well as committing the Quran to memory. Indeed, the ending of *Fahrenheit 451*, where people are trained and checked in their memorization of books bears a striking resemblance to Quran classes in madrasahs.

During the holy month of Ramadan, tarawih prayers are read in mosques every evening. Tarawih prayers include Quran recitation. Any hafith who stumbles is sure to be corrected by another hafith.

A number of scholars point to hadiths that state that a hafith will be rewarded on the Day of Judgement, as will his or her parents, and will be granted the ability to intercede on behalf of ten family members:

> Whoever reads the Quran and memorizes it, while he regards what it makes lawful as lawful and its unlawful as forbidden [i.e. he practices according to it], Allah will admit him into Jannah and will accept his intercession on behalf of ten such persons of his family who were doomed to the fire of Jahannam (At-Tirmithi).

The memorization of the Quran was very important to Muslims in the past and is also in the present. Yearly, many students master the Quran and complete the book with understanding (*tafsir*) and also memorization. One group of people in the Middle East who often become hafiths is prisoners. They are native speakers of Arabic, which makes memorizing it easier. They have a lot of spare time on their hands. And, God willing, insha Allah, they realize the error of their ways, and feel that memorizing the Quran is a way of repenting for their past sins and turning over a new leaf.

Muhammad was known as "the walking Quran"; that is, he had memorized the whole Quran and was a perfect example of how to live our lives according to it. There is no better way to follow Islam than to memorize the Quran.

It is impossible to give a precise figure for the number of hafiths in today's world. One figure often quoted is 10 million. Over the past centuries, it must run into many millions.

1 Christianity in View (2022). Statistics and forecasts for world religions: 1800-2025. *Christianity in View.* http://christianityinview.com/religion-statistics.html

4

Islamic Terms and Concepts

Islamic Terms and Concepts

We have already touched on the fact that Arabic is Arabic, and English is English, and translations can never fully cover all the nuances of the original. For example, in Chapter 2, we saw that the English word *prayer* covers two different activities in Islam: the five daily prayers (*salah*) and any other supplication (*dua*).

Similarly, in Chapter 10, the word *charity* was seen to cover two different types: compulsory charity (*zakah*) – and there are two types of *zakah* – and any other charity (*sadaqah*).

Likewise, in Chapter 11, the Hajj pilgrimage to Makkah was described. Any Muslim going to Makkah and performing similar required activities at any other time of year, is doing Umrah, not Hajj. However, both Hajj and Umrah would have to be translated as *pilgrimage* in English.

Other Arabic Islamic terms and concepts that are difficult to translate into English – especially as one-word English equivalents – are explained in this section.

The two Arabic words that are most regularly mistranslated with negative connotations, and therefore misunderstood, are *jihad* and *fatwa*. *Jihad* does not unequivocally mean "holy war", and *fatwa* does not mean "death sentence." However, that is how these concepts are often presented in English translation.

Most people have heard of halal food, but would be hard put to explain exactly what the process of making it halal involves. And most people are unaware that halal does not relate just to food, but to all activities that a Muslim may carry out in their daily life.

These and other Arabic words (*Islam, ibadah, kafir, haqq*) are clarified in this section. Many such words cannot be easily translated by a single English word, and therefore need a clumsy phrase to convey the meaning, which even then may not convey all the overtones of the Arabic. For this reason, many Muslims simply use the Arabic word when talking about Islam in English.

23 Problems of translation

The number of Arabic speakers worldwide (both native and non-native) is over 400 million. While this makes Arabic the fifth most commonly-spoken language in the world today, it still represents less than 5% of the world population. In short, the vast majority of the world population does not know Arabic. As a result, most people wanting to learn about Islam by reading the Quran, will have to start by reading a translation into a language they know.

As anyone who knows a foreign language well is aware, there are various problems associated with translation. The grammatical structures of different languages differ. Language reflects culture, and thus cultural differences come into play. Words may have more than one meaning, and overtones – a particular problem with Arabic. Translators may or may not want to stick as closely as possible to the language and style of the original. Some English translators of the Quran felt obliged to emulate the archaic English of the 1611 King James version of the Bible. Translators need to make practical decisions on questions such as these.

Some of these problems can be illustrated by examining translations of Surat al-Ikhlas (#112): "(In the name of God, the Gracious, the Merciful.) Say: 'He is God, the One. God, the Absolute. He begets not, nor was He begotten, and there is none comparable to Him.'"

Reciting

The first thing to notice is that many Muslims when reciting the Quran do so by chanting it in a musical way. This may strike many non-Muslims as strange, as other holy books, such as the Bible, are normally simply read. So, many non-Arabic speakers may be surprised to hear the Quran recited musically.

The Bismillah *opening*

Every chapter of the Quran (except #9) starts with the phrase *Bismillah ir-rahman ir-rahim*. It is translated as "In the name of God" followed by two adjectives, *rahman* and *rahim*. These adjectives are variously translated into English as "gracious, merciful, mercy-giving, beneficent, compassionate", and more.

In Arabic, they are intensive forms of these adjectives, i.e. they are stronger than simply "gracious, merciful". They are therefore often translated as "most gracious, most merciful". However, this implies a comparison with others (that is, God is more merciful than all others). We are thus starting to compare God with others, such as humans, and this is something we should avoid (known in Arabic as *shirk*).

Both *rahman* and *rahim* are derived from the Semitic root *r – h - m* which indicates something of the utmost tenderness which provides protection and nourishment, and that from which all of creation is brought into being. And indeed, the root *r – h - m* has meanings of "womb, kinship, relationship, loving-kindness, mercy, compassion, and nourishing tenderness". Rahman is only applied to God, but the attribute rahim is a more general term, and may also be applied to humans. This is a distinction that no English words can capture.

The –ad *ending*

Each of the four verses of the chapter ends in *–ad* (*ahad, samad, yulad, ahad*). This ending makes the surah sound definite, axiomatic, self-evident and beyond discussion. This is in contrast to other surahs, where the ayah ending is less definite, as it is more persuasive in nature. Again, no English words can capture this.

Qul

Qul means "say". It is easily translated, although non-Arabic readers may need to understand what this means. T. B. Irving, in commentary on his translation of the Quran[1], says that this surah "forms an answer to a previous rhetorical question implied in the first word, which is 'Say'". That is, it is as if it is an answer to the question "What should I say when people ask me what God is like?" For this reason, translations often include the understood addressee: "Say [O Muhammad]."

He

Scholars of Tafsir and Classical Arabic explain that while huwa is often translated as "he" it actually is a third-person, singular pronoun that refers to something that is known to all, but ambiguous and not identified with any. However, there is always the problem of using pronouns to refer to God (see Chapter 3).

Allah

The word *Allah* is often translated as "God" with a capital G. However, capital letters are a feature of English, but many other languages, such as Arabic, Hebrew, Devanagari and Thai, have no distinction between capital and lower-case letters. Also, the English word *god* can be made plural (*gods*), and made feminine (*goddess*), but this is not possible in Arabic. For this reason, many translators leave the word *Allah* untranslated.

Initial capitals

As explained in Chapter 3, it is conventional in English to use an initial capital for an epithet (noun or adjective) or pronoun referring to God, e.g. *the Absolute, Him*. This can be done in English, but corresponds to nothing in the original, as Arabic has no capital letters.

Ahad

God is *ahad*, sometimes translated simply as "One". The word ahad is also translated as "the one and only; the only one; unique". It is different from the Arabic word *wahid*, which is the everyday word for "one" when counting. *Wahid* "one" is followed by *ithnan* "two", *thalatha* "three", and *arbaa* "four". *Ahad*, on the other hand, also means "one, but there is no two, three, or four". This cannot be expressed in English, which only has one word: one.

Samad

Samad is a difficult word to translate because, like many Arabic words, it has more than one meaning or overtone. It is variously translated as "the Eternal, Absolute", "the eternally Besought of all", "the Source for everything", and amongst others "the everlasting Refuge". Abdullah Yusuf Ali, in commentary in his translation of the Quran[2], says, about *samad*: "… absolute existence can only be predicated of Him; all other existence is temporal or conditional, … He is dependent on no person or things, but all persons or things are dependent on Him, thus negating the idea of gods and goddesses who ate and drank, wrangled and plotted, depended on gifts of worshipers, etc."

This is of course difficult to put into one English word. Perhaps *self-sufficient* is the nearest. Some translations leave the word untranslated, with an explanation, e.g. "The Self-Sufficient Master, Whom all creatures need. He neither eats nor drinks."

Beget

The third ayah is often translated "He begetteth not, nor is He begotten." However, English dictionaries tell us that this verb *beget* is old-fashioned, formal, and used in religious contexts. Certainly the *–th* ending of *begetteth* is equally old-fashioned. More modern translations use phrases such as *He has not fathered anyone nor was he fathered.* Of course, skeptics will again say that this use of father implies that God is male. Or *He does not give birth and He is not born from anyone.* Again, skeptics will say that this implies that God is female, because *give birth* is normally used of mothers.

In everyday English we might say: "He is nobody's father, and nobody's son" or, sex-neutrally: "He is nobody's parent, and nobody's child."

This ayah is an unequivocal negation of the Christian concept of a God the Father, and God the Son.

Final ayah

The final ayah is in fact the simplest to translate without difficulty into English: "And there is nothing comparable to Him." While this is the easiest ayah to translate, it is no less significant in meaning. It sums up the whole argument of the surah. Indeed, the whole surah was described by Muhammad as being equal to one-third of the Quran, because it covers succinctly the major concepts of Islam, namely the existence and nature of God, especially that we should acknowledge his Oneness (tauhid) and avoid associating others with Him (shirk) by suggesting that they are on a par with Him.

Like many chapters and verses in the Quran, Surat al-Ikhlas is short and deceptively simple-seeming. It is short: you can read it in ten seconds. But it is full of meaning, and as a result, is not easy to translate adequately. For this reason, it is important for Muslims to learn some Arabic, and to memorize parts of the Quran in its original Arabic (see Chapter 22).

1 Irving, T. B. (1988). *The Qur'an: The first American version* (3rd edition). Amana Books.

2 Abdullah Yusuf Ali (1934). *The holy Qur'an: Text, translation and commentary.* Shaik Muhammad Ashraf Publishers. https://wikilivres.org/wiki/The_Holy_Qur%27an

24 Jihad

This chapter deals with the Arabic word that is probably the most mistranslated and misunderstood. The word is *jihad*.

Inaccurate dictionary definitions

A non-Muslim wanting to know the meaning of this word would understandably consult an English dictionary. However, this would not be helpful, as many dictionaries only give a definition of "holy war", e.g. "A war fought by Muslims to defend or spread their beliefs" (*The Britannica Dictionary*).

This is also the definitional equivalent used by the United States Department of Justice, which:

> has used its own ad hoc definitions of *jihad* in indictments of individuals involved in terrorist activities: "As used in this First Superseding Indictment, *Jihad* is the Arabic word meaning 'holy war'. In this context, *jihad* refers to the use of violence, including paramilitary action against persons, governments deemed to be enemies of the fundamentalist version of Islam."[1]

It is thus not surprising if non-Muslims have an inaccurate understanding of the word *jihad*, to mean war and fighting. From a purely linguistic point of view, anyone who knows the Arabic language knows that this is wrong. The Arabic word for "war" is *harb*. When the Quran talks about fighting, it uses the Arabic word *qital* (not *jihad*).

> "Fight (*qatilu*) in the cause of God, and know that God is Hearing and Knowing" (2.244).

Jihad, on the other hand, is much broader in scope. It is often translated as "strife, struggle, endeavor, effort, exertion", with no overtones at all of fighting.

> "The believers are those who believe in God and His Messenger, and then have not doubted, and strive (*jahadu*) for God's cause with their wealth and their persons. These are the sincere" (49:15).

Arabic etymology and definition

The meaning of the Arabic noun *jihad*, which comes from the verb *juhud*, is "striving, struggling, a determined effort". In this literal sense, all Muslims perform jihad, because they are commanded to strive in the way of God. In this sense, to "declare jihad" is meaningless; jihad is a struggle you perform, not something you declare.

Iraqi-born Majid Khadduri, professor at Indiana, Chicago and Johns Hopkins universities, lists four kinds of struggle in the cause of God (jihad fi sabilillah)[2]:

1. Jihad of the heart (*jihad bil qalb/nafs*) is concerned with combatting the devil and in the attempt to escape his persuasion to evil. This type of jihad was regarded as the greater jihad (*al-jihad al-akbar*).
2. Jihad by the tongue (*jihad bil lisan*) (also jihad by the word, *jihad al-qalam*) is concerned with speaking the truth and spreading the word of Islam with one's tongue.
3. Jihad by the hand (*jihad bil yad*) refers to choosing to do what is right and to combat injustice and what is wrong with action.
4. Jihad by the sword (*jihad bis saif*) refers to *qital fi sabilillah* (armed fighting in the way of God, or holy war).

This categorization is reminiscent of the hadith in which Prophet Muhammad (pbuh) said: "If one of you sees something wrong, let him change it with his hand; if he cannot, then with his tongue; if he cannot, then with his heart and this is the weakest faith" (Muslim). Some versions add: "… there is no part of faith behind that, not even so much as a mustard seed." Note that this hadith does not mention violence.

Jihad may, under particular circumstances, involve fighting. However, armed jihad (fighting) is labelled the lesser jihad, while peaceful jihad is called the greater jihad.

It is worth remembering that 6th-7th century CE Arabia was a time of vengeance, aggression and war between tribes. After one such battle, "a number of fighters came to Muhammad and he said: 'You have come from the lesser jihad to the greater jihad.' The fighters asked: 'What is the greater jihad?' Muhammad replied: 'It is the struggle against one's passions.'" (narrated by Al-Bayhaqi, Al-Khatib, Ibn Taymiyyah and others, although some scholars regard this hadith as being of dubious reliability[3]). In other words, fighting is very much secondary to the struggle against your passions.

The Arabic word for your passions is *nafs*, literally meaning "soul", but in this context also translated as "lower self, base desires, animal instincts, inferior drives, evil motives, ego". The greater jihad is thus your struggle against these base desires.

Jihad is a term that is misused by people on all sides. This led the Egyptian-born American Muslim leader, Dr. Maher Hathout, to write a book *Jihad vs. Terrorism*[4,5], to set the record straight for two reasons:

> Number one was the discovery that everyone is defining us except us, everyone is explaining jihad except for Muslims. Second, I noticed that some Muslims needed to brush up, to review the issue on their own for clarity and understanding of their own religion. This is why I made the book very textual. I tried to use verses from the Koran, from the Prophet … It includes personal opinion of course, but the backbone is textual.[4]

Peaceful jihad (greater jihad)

Peaceful jihad is thus against your nafs. There are many verses in the Quran, and hadiths, explaining the concept further.

Peaceful jihad may be no more than speaking up against evil. "The best jihad is the word of justice in front of the oppressive sultan" (Ibn Habban).

The importance of preaching the word of Islam is emphasized in the Quran. "Had We willed, We could have sent to every town a warner. So do not obey the disbelievers, but strive (*jahidhum*) against them with it [the Quran], a mighty struggle (*jihadan*)" (25:51-52).

Muhammad even considered serving one's parents as being a higher goal than armed jihad. "A man came to the Prophet asking permission to wage [armed] jihad. The Prophet asked: 'Are your parents alive?' The man replied: 'Yes.' The Prophet advised: 'Then strive in the service of them both'" (Bukhari, Muslim).

Muhammad even considered performing Hajj a superior activity to armed jihad. "The best jihad [for women] is Hajj mabrur [Hajj that is accepted by God, because it is performed perfectly]" (Bukhari).

It is emphasized that striving to obey God – by following his instructions as contained in the Quran and hadiths – is jihad, and the means of achieving success. Submitting to the will of God is the literal meaning of the word *Islam*.

> "O you who believe! Be conscious of God, and seek the means of approach to Him, and strive (*jahidu*) in His cause, so that you may succeed" (5:35).

> "The *mujahid* [person who does jihad] is he who does jihad against his lower self in obeying Allah, the Mighty, the Sublime" (At-Tirmithi).

In many places in the Quran, the concept of believing is juxtaposed with the concept of doing righteous deeds. It has even been claimed[6] that:

> ... the term *righteous deeds* is almost synonymous with the term *jihad*, though each emphasizes different aspects of those deeds. The term *jihad* stresses the fact that these deeds are not things that the human is naturally inclined to or easily accepts, so the emphasis is on the struggle involved. For instance, making a habit of donating one's money and giving it to the needy, rather than using it to seek personal pleasures and worldly riches, is not something that the person feels comfortable with.

Armed jihad (lesser jihad)

In Makkah, the early Muslims were being persecuted for their beliefs. They therefore migrated to Madinah (known at that time as Yathrib) at the invitation of the inhabitants. During all this time, the Muslims did not fight back, but suffered hardships, because no revelation permitting them to fight (and shed human blood) had been given by God. A couple of years after the Hijrah migration, before the Battle of Badr, this permission was granted by the following revelation: "Permission [to fight] is given to those who are fought against, and God is Able to give them victory. Those who were unjustly evicted from their homes, merely for saying, 'Our Lord is God'" (22:39-40).

God granted this permission, but it came with many conditions. Firstly, as the above verses show, the Muslims should only fight against those who had waged war against them and driven them out of their homes in Makkah. Armed jihad is therefore self-defense, not offensive.

After the Battle of Badr, the following verse was revealed regarding enemies who renege on promises, ceasefires and treaties.

> If you fear treachery on the part of a people, break off with them in a like manner. God does not like the treacherous. … And prepare against them all the power you can muster, and all the cavalry you can mobilize, to terrify thereby God's enemies and your enemies, and others besides them whom you do not know, but God knows them. … But if they incline towards peace, then incline towards it, and put your trust in God (8:58).

This verse spells out that armed jihad is intended only to produce peace between the sides. So, the response from the Muslim side should be proportional to the force of the attack, and no more. This is also mentioned in 2:194: "[Fighting in] The sacred month [is] for [aggression committed in] the sacred month; and sacrilege calls for retaliation. Whoever commits aggression against you, retaliate against him in the same measure as he has committed against you."

The mention of a sacred month reminds us that four of the 12 months in the Islamic calendar are considered sacred: Rajab (#7), Thu al-Qadah (11), Thu al-Hijjah (12) and Muharram (1). During these months, fighting (armed jihad) is forbidden, unless you are attacked. This means that Muslims are forbidden to fight in one-third of their lives.

When the Muslims returned to Makkah from Madinah, eight years after the Hijrah, the Quraish continued their persecution of them. This episode is often referred to as the "conquest" of Makkah; however, it was a peaceful conquest. Muhammad issued an amnesty for all the people of Makkah, apart from 17. Thirteen of them were eventually pardoned, but four of them were killed for particularly heinous crimes.

Hind bint Utbah was an opponent of Islam who, at the Battle of Uhud, hired a slave to kill Hamzah, Muhammad's uncle, with a spear, and she cut out his liver. Even Hind was pardoned. Indeed, her husband, Abu Sufian, a prominent Quraish, converted to Islam shortly after, despite his original bitter enmity towards the Muslims. And so did Hind.

The fact that the Makkans had prohibited Muhammad from going to Masjid al-Haram in Makkah to perform Hajj while he was in Madinah, did not lead to retribution. The following verse gives the instruction: "And let not the hatred of people who barred you from the Sacred Mosque incite you to aggression. And cooperate with one another in virtuous conduct and conscience, and do not cooperate with one another in sin and hostility" (5:2).

In the end, Muhammad only performed Hajj once, after the conquest of Makkah.

Islam has strict rules for the conduct of armed jihad:

- It is not "no holds barred" fighting, but conducted in a disciplined way, without anger.
- It avoids hurting non-combatants, e.g. women, children, old people, monks.
- It is conducted with the minimum necessary force, to repel aggression.
- Prisoners of war are treated humanely.
- Dead bodies are not mutilated.
- Trees and crops should not be harmed, chopped down or burned.
- The educational value of prisoners of war was understood. Literate POWs could secure their freedom by teaching ten Muslims to read and write.

Summary

The similarities and differences between peaceful greater jihad and armed lesser jihad are summarized in the table below:

Peaceful greater jihad	Armed lesser jihad
Against an internal enemy	Against an external enemy
Self-defense against your nafs and Satan	Self-defense against those who wage war, drive Muslims from their homes, from their land, steal possessions, renege on treaties, etc.
Intended to improve oneself	Intended to repel aggression
Intended to bring peace	Intended to bring peace
Permanent, for continual improvement	Temporary, while aggression persists
A 24/7/52 activity	Forbidden one-third of the year
Follows on from belief (iman), obeying God	Follows on from belief (iman), obeying God
Rules regarding halal and haram activities	Rules regarding halal and haram activities
Relates to everyday activities	Relates to out-of-the-ordinary circumstances, that may never occur
Every Muslim should be continually trying to become a better Muslim. So, every Muslim should perform peaceful jihad throughout their life.	If there is no aggression, there is no need for armed jihad. A Muslim may thus go through their whole life without performing armed jihad.

Advertisement campaigns

In 2012, pro-Israel activists in the USA put an advertisement on buses, subway trains, and other places with the text: "In any war between the civilized man and the savage, support the civilized man. Support Israel. Defeat jihad."

The advertisement was criticized, not only by Muslims because of the deliberate misinterpretation of *jihad*, but also by others. Bloomberg[7] called it a "shitty ad" by implying that Muslims are savages.

Muslims in the USA countered with the following series of advertisements, with examples of the correct meaning of *jihad*: *My jihad is to stay fit despite my busy schedule; My jihad is to not judge people by their cover; My jihad is to march on despite losing my son; My jihad is to never settle short of my best effort; My jihad is to build friendships across the aisle.*

Positive connotations

Thus the word *jihad* means peaceful jihad for the vast majority of Muslims, who never have occasion in their lives to perform armed jihad. The word *jihad* is thus a word with positive connotations for Muslims, relating to the individual's lifelong endeavor to become a better Muslim and a better person. For this reason, *jihad* can be a Muslim name. For example, Jihad Abdo is one of Syria's best-known actors. However, because of the unjustified western overemphasis on the lesser "holy war" sense of jihad, many Muslims find their given name problematical; Jihad Abdo uses the stage name Jay Abdo in Hollywood.

Dictionary definitions

If a non-Muslim is confused, and wants to find out the meaning of the word *jihad*, an understandable practice is to look the word up in a dictionary or similar reference book. However, this may not clarify the situation, as the definitions given are often wide of the mark. We can distinguish five types of definition.

1. Only armed jihad

Some dictionaries only give the "holy war" sense which, as we have shown above, is a minor sense, and one not held by Muslims.

"A holy war undertaken by Muslims against unbelievers" (Oxford Reference)

2. Armed jihad, peaceful jihad

Some dictionaries give both senses, but with the lesser "holy war" sense first.

"A holy war waged on behalf of Islam as a religious duty. *Also*: a personal struggle in devotion to Islam especially involving spiritual discipline" (*Merriam-Webster Dictionary*)

3. Peaceful jihad, armed jihad

Some dictionaries have the definitions just about right, with the greater jihad first, and the lesser second.

"In Islam, a religious struggle against evil in yourself or in society. A holy war fought by Muslims against people who are a threat to Islam" (*Cambridge Dictionary*)

4. Only peaceful jihad

These definitions contain no mention of fighting.

"The personal struggle of the individual believer against evil and persecution. A struggle undertaken by Muslims in defense of the Islamic faith" (*Collins English Dictionary*)

5. Discussion of misunderstanding and mistranslation

While the *Britannica Dictionary*, quoted above, gives the "holy war" sense, the *Encyclopedia Britannica* sets the record straight:

> A meritorious struggle or effort. The exact meaning of the term *jihad* depends on context; it has often been erroneously translated in the West as "holy war". Jihad, particularly in the religious and ethical realm, primarily refers to the human struggle to promote what is right and to prevent what is wrong.

Muslims would be comfortable with #3, 4 and 5 above, but #1 and 2 perpetuate the myth that *jihad* primarily means fighting.

To conclude, we might quote *National Geographic Magazine* again[5]: "*Jihad* is a loaded term - and a concept that illustrates a deep gulf of miscommunication between Islam and the West. There are those in each community who see jihad as a clash of civilizations - and act on those beliefs." While most Muslims interpret the term overwhelmingly in a non-violent sense, "it is the jihad of the sword that has received the lion's share of global attention."

Perhaps the tide is changing, and the correct interpretation of *jihad* is being adopted in the West. A 2020 report[8] relates to the UK National Association of Muslim Police (NAMP), which has over 3,000 members. An online conference addressed by the London Metropolitan Police Assistant Commissioner Neil Basu, head of counterterrorism policing, discussed the use of terms like *Islamist terror* and *jihadi*, regularly used by UK media.

The NAMP complained that the use of terms like *Islamist terror* that "have a direct link to Islam and jihad ... do not help community relations and public confidence," arguing they instead contribute to discrimination, Islamophobia, and negative perceptions of Muslims. Instead, they want attackers motivated by religious ideology to be described with the Arabic word *irhabi*, used in the Middle East to describe extremist views – or, if a substitute English term is desired, as *faith-claimed terrorism*. Predictably, the proposal was met with mockery from UK Islamophobes brought up on western media terminology.

Metropolitan Police Chief Superintendent Nik Adams said that, while the police force had no immediate plans to adopt the NAMP's recommendations for relabeling these offenders, it was "vital" that they settle upon the best terminology to "define the threat accurately and succinctly but also to avoid alienating communities crucial to our efforts".

1 Wikipedia (n.d.). *Jihad*. https://en.wikipedia.org/wiki/Jihad

2 Khadduri, M. (2010). *War and peace in the law of Islam*. The Lawbook Exchange (Originally published by Johns Hopkins Press, 1955).

3 BBC (2014). *Jihad*. https://www.bbc.co.uk/religion/religions/islam/beliefs/jihad_1.shtml

4 Hathout, M. (2002). *Jihad vs. terrorism*. Dawn Books. https://archive.org/details/jihadvsterrorism0000hath/mode/2up

5 Handwerk, B. (2003). What does "jihad" really mean to Muslims? *National Geographic News*, 24 October, 2003. https://www.nationalgeographic.com/culture/article/what-does-jihad-really-mean-to-muslims

6 Louay Fatoohi (2004). *Jihad in the Qur'an: The truth from the course*. A. S. Noordeen.

7 Badger, E. (2012). Yes, this ad is offensive. But free speech rides public transit, too. *Bloomberg*, 6 October 2012. https://www.bloomberg.com/news/articles/2012-10-05/yes-this-ad-is-offensive-but-free-speech-rides-public-transit-too

8 RT (2020). *Jihadi no more? UK police mull ditching 'Islamist terror' & similar phrases after complaints from Muslim cops.* https://www.rt.com/uk/495336-uk-police-islamist-terror-terminology

25 Islam

It has become a commonplace habit that, when an act of terrorism is perpetrated by someone claiming to be Muslim, they are described in the media as an "Islamic terrorist", but when the act is perpetrated by someone claiming to be from a different religion, they are a "lone wolf".

It is therefore gratifying that in 2021 the Australian Security Intelligence Organization (ASIO)[1] dropped the use of the term Islamic extremism (along with left-wing and right-wing extremism). Instead, the terms "religiously motivated violent extremism" and "ideologically motivated violent extremism" would be used.

ASIO Head, Mike Burgess, said the old terms did not "adequately describe the phenomena we're seeing". He pointed out that it is violence that the organisation investigates, rather than the motivation behind the violence:

> ASIO does not investigate people solely because of their political views. … In the same way, we don't investigate people because of their religious views. Again, it's violence that is relevant to our powers, but that's not always clear when we use the term "Islamic extremism".

He said some Muslim groups understandably saw the term Islamic extremism as "damaging and misrepresentative of Islam", and stigmatizing them "by encouraging stereotyping and stoking division".

Islamic extremism

The term *Islamic extremism* is in fact an oxymoron, i.e. self-contradictory. In various places in the Quran, God (Allah) states that Muslims should avoid extremism but instead follow the straight path of moderation. "Thus We made you a moderate community" (2:143). Similarly, in several hadiths, Prophet Muhammad (pbuh) iterated the same sentiment. "Always adopt a middle, moderate, regular course, whereby you will reach your target [of Paradise]" (Bukhari).

Terrorism and extremism are in no way a directive of the Quran, hadiths, or any other Islamic literature. Muslims therefore reject the very idea of Islamic terrorism or extremism. They are the very opposite of Islam.

Meaning of Islam

The Arabic word Islam is used by God in the Quran to refer to the religion. One of the last verses revealed to Muhammad states: "Today I have perfected your religion for you, and have completed My favor upon you, and have approved Islam as a religion for you" (5:3).

The Arabic word for what is usually translated as "religion" is *din*. However, it is better translated as "way of life", as it encompasses all aspects of religious and everyday life. The word *din* also means "judgement". In the first surah of the Quran (al-Fatihah), God describes Himself as the Master of the Day of Judgement (*din*), the Day of Resurrection when people's deeds in this life will be judged.

Like many Arabic words, *Islam* has more than one meaning. Its basic meaning is "submission to the will of God, and obedience to His guidance". In Arabic, consonants are much more important than vowels, as they show relationships between words from the same root. The *s – l – m* root in Islam also occurs in *salam*, meaning "peace", as in the everyday Muslim greeting *As-salamu alaikum* "Peace be upon you". The root also occurs in *salama*, meaning "wellbeing". Thus, Muslims find peace and wellbeing by following God's instructions.

The phrase translated as "I have approved Islam as a religion for you" probably meant something rather different for the early Muslims from how it sounds today in translation. Nowadays, it sounds like: "If you have a census form, and it asks for your religion – Buddhism / Christianity / Hinduism / Islam / Judaism / etc. – then tick the 'Islam' box." However, as we have just explained, Islam was not an established world religion at that time, but rather meant "acknowledgement of one God (*tauhid*) and submission to Him". Similarly, din meant "way of life, daily conduct". So this verse rather means: "I have chosen submission to Me [God] according to the guidelines in this Quran, and my Prophet Muhammad's Sunnah, as the way you should conduct your daily life."

Names of religions

So that is the meaning of the word *Islam*, used as the name of the religion. Given that it is related to the word *salam*, meaning "peace", detractors who say that Islam is a violent religion evidently know little about Islam.

It has often been pointed out that most religions are named after a person or place.

Bahai: after Husayn Ali (1817 – 1892), known as Bahaullah ("splendor of God").

Buddhism: after Siddhartha Gautama (6th or 5th century BCE), known as the Buddha ("the awakened/enlightened one").

Christianity: after Jesus (Isa), whom Christians believe to be the Son of God. The word *Christ* is often misunderstood. "Sometimes I have to tell my students that Christ was not Jesus's last name. … Christ is a title and is, in fact, the Greek translation of the Hebrew word for messiah."[2] *Christ* means "anointed with oil" and was used of kings, prophets and priests, to show their religious status. However, the same word is also used for inanimate objects: "I *am* the God of Bethel, where thou anointedst the pillar" (Genesis 31:13). When used to refer to Jesus, Christ is nowadays spelled in English with an initial capital C, although this practice only started in the 14th century CE, and was not fixed until the 17th. Before that, the Old English word *hæland* meaning "healer, savior" was used.

Confucianism: after the 6th – 5th century BCE Chinese philosopher Kung Fu-tzu, Latinized as Confucius.

Hinduism: from the Sanskrit *Sindhu* referring to the Indus River (in present-day Pakistan). The Arabic *al-Hind* and Persian *Hindu* referred to those people living beyond the Indus River.

Judaism: from Judah, the fourth son of Jacob (Yakub).

Zoroastrianism: from Zoroaster, a pre-5th century BCE prophet in Persia (modern Iran). His date and place of birth are an unknown matter of debate.

The hazy origins of four other major world religions, and their names, are as follows.

Jainism: from the Sanskrit *jinah* "saint, overcomer". The religion dates to the 6th century BCE, although it is not known who started it.

Shinto: "way of the gods" from Chinese *shin* "god(s)" and *tao* "way". It "is Japan's native belief system and predates historical records."[3]

Sikhism: founded around 1500 by Guru Nanak (1469-1539) in Punjab, India, and led subsequently by nine other gurus. The word *sikh* comes from Hindi and Sanskrit, meaning "student". The Sikhs call their faith Gurmat (Punjabi for "the way of the guru").

Taoism: from Chinese *tao* "way". "Taoism has been connected to the philosopher Lao Tzu, who around 500 BCE wrote the main book of Taoism, the Tao Te Ching."[4]

Muhammadanism

A term that has been used to refer to the religion of Islam by non-Muslims, especially Christians, is *Muhammadanism*. This word was produced by analogy with *Christianity*: (Jesus) *Christ* > *Christianity*, *Muhammad* > *Muhammadanism*. This misunderstanding dates back at least to the 13th century CE.

The word *Muhammadanism*, implying that Muhammad is worshiped as if he were a god, the way Christians worship Jesus, is nowadays thoroughly discredited. There are several Muslim objections to it.

Firstly, Muhammad himself never used such a term. On the contrary, he emphasized that he was just a messenger: "Indeed messengerhood and prophethood have been terminated, so there shall be no messenger after me, nor a prophet" (At-Tirmithi).

Secondly, in the Quran (33:40), God states the same message: "Muhammad is not the father of any of your men; but he is the Messenger of God, and the seal of the prophets. God is Cognizant of everything."

Thirdly, in the Quran (33:21), God emphasizes the importance of following the Sunnah of Muhammad, as a messenger: "You have an excellent example in the Messenger of God; for anyone who seeks God and the Last Day, and remembers God frequently."

Fourthly, in the Quran (20:14), God, as its "author," reminds its readers to worship Him, and not Muhammad: "I am God. There is no God but I. So serve Me, and practice the prayer for My remembrance."

Finally, Muhammad emphasized that he was just a human being, a man, who did all the everyday things that men do:

> I swear by Allah that I am the most fearful of Allah and most conscious of Him than all of you. But I also fast and break my fast, pray and sleep, and I marry women. Whoever turns away from my Sunnah is not from me [one of the true followers] (Bukhari).

In short, all Muslims worship God, and no Muslims worship Muhammad. Several times each day, Muslims repeat the declaration of faith that reconfirms this: "I declare that there is nothing worthy of worship but God, and Muhammad is the messenger of God."

Terrorists

As noted above, *Islamic extremism* and *Muslim terrorism* are terms widely used in the western media for atrocities carried out by people claiming to be representing the religion of Islam. As explained above, extremism and terrorism have nothing to do with Islam, whose literal *s – l – m* meaning is "peace".

In an article entitled "Propaganda and Islam: What you're not being told", Justin King[5] debunks many of the myths that are regularly propagated by non-Muslims about Islam and Muslims. This all relates to propaganda. As King explains:

> Propaganda is the wheel by which the government steers the bus of a nation; typically driving it into war or off the cliff of humanity. It is amazing to see how many people who are otherwise rational human beings will blindly follow the herd on the matter of how subhuman a perceived national enemy is. The western media wonderfully paints Islam as a death cult bent on world domination. Over and over again the American populace is shown footage of the atrocities committed by fanatics or of Arab men burning American flags. The problem, of course, is that this isn't remotely representative of the Islamic population of the world.

In 2010, Fox Host Brian Kilmeade used the catchphrase "Not all Muslims are terrorists, but all terrorists are Muslims" to defend the remark by political commentator Bill O'Reilly, against the proposed mosque in the rebuilt World Trade Center, that "Muslims attacked us on 9/11"[6]. They added: "It wasn't just one person, it was religion", implying that the bombers were not lone wolves, but representative of mainstream Islam. In contrast to Kilmeade and O'Reilly's comments, implying that the 9/11 attacks represented Islam, the Organization of Islamic Cooperation (OIC), which represents 57 member states, immediately denounced the attacks as "brutal" and contrary to Islamic teachings. This was not widely reported.

The statistics show conclusively that Muslims are not terrorists. Of all the "terrorist" attacks in the USA, two-thirds were perpetrated by far-right groups in 2019, and 90% in 2020[7]. In the European Union, the great majority of "terrorist" attacks since 2010 have been carried out by separatist groups[8]. In 2021, there were only 15 such attacks in the EU. As Statista[9] point out: "To put this in a global context, the country with the most terrorist attacks, Afghanistan, suffered 1,722 attacks in 2020, followed by Syria which had 1,332."

King[5] quotes similar figures to debunk the "Muslims are terrorists" and other claims that are well wide of the mark.

It is also easy to find instances of terrorism from people purporting to belong to other world religions:

Protestantism: On 18 June 1984, David Lane and Bruce Pierce killed liberal Denver-based Jewish talk show host Alan Berg, a critic of white supremacists, with an automatic weapon. Lane was a former Ku Klux Klan member. The Ku Klux Klan, who claim to uphold Christian values, were reportedly responsible for the murder of three of Malcolm X's father's brothers, and the Black Legion, a similar white supremacist group, for the murder of his father.

Catholicism: The Irish Republican Army (IRA) rose from the Catholic side of the Catholic vs Protestant divide in Ireland. Since the early 20th century CE, they have carried out regular acts of terrorism, including the infamous London bombings of the 1970s. Indeed, while the 7 July 2005 bombings by "Islamists" are often quoted in a list of terrorist incidents in London, the great majority have been carried out by the IRA, Scottish nationalists, and other political groups.

Hinduism: Dara Singh is a member of the Hindu Bajrang Dal organization (he is not a Sikh), and led the murder of Australian Christian missionary Graham Staines and his two sons, by burning them alive in their station wagon in Kendujhar, Orissa, on 22 January 1999.

Buddhism: In June 2014, Buddhist monks not merely participated in, but actually led, attacks on Muslim property in Sri Lanka. It is estimated that nine shops, forty homes, and three mosques were attacked. At least three people were killed and 75 severely wounded.

Judaism: Israel was established in 1948, with at least 18 massacres of Palestinians, including Deir Yassin and Balad Al-Shaykh[10].

The word used for the religion, by God, Muhammad, and Muslims worldwide, is *Islam*, meaning "submission". The word for its adherents is *Muslims*; it is a related word (note the *s – l – m*) meaning "one who submits". The adjective in English is either *Islamic* or *Muslim*.

Muslim terrorism and *Islamic extremism* are oxymorons, as Islam promotes peace and moderation. Muslims dissociate themselves from violent acts of terrorism, in the same way that Christians dissociate themselves from the Ku Klux Klan, or Catholics from the IRA.

1 Grattan, M. (2021). ASIO to avoid "left", "right" and "Islamic" in an overhaul of its descriptions of extremism. *Australasian Muslim Times*, 18 March 2021. www.amust.com.au/2021/03/asio-to-avoid-left-right-and-islamic-in-an-overhaul-of-its-descriptions-of-extremism

2 Ehrman, B. D. (2014). *How Jesus became God*. HarperOne.

3 Online Etymology Dictionary (n.d.). *Shinto*. https://www.etymonline.com/word/shinto

4 National Geographic (n.d.). *Taoism*. https://education.nationalgeographic.org/resource/taoism/

5 King, J. (2014). Propaganda and Islam: What you're not being told. *The Anti-Media*. https://themindunleashed.com/2020/01/islam-propaganda.html

6 Millican, J., Berrier, J. & Schroeck, E. (2010). Kilmeade makes outrageous and

obviously false claim that "all terrorists are Muslims". *Media Matters for America*, 15 October 2010. https://www.mediamatters.org/fox-friends/kilmeade-makes-outrageous-and-obviously-false-claim-all-terrorists-are-muslims

7 Wilson, J. (2020). Violence by far right is among US's most dangerous terrorist threats, study finds. *The Guardian*, 27 June 2020. https://www.theguardian.com/world/2020/jun/27/us-far-right-violence-terrorist-threat-analysis

8 Statista (n.d.). *Number of failed, foiled or completed terrorist attacks in the European Union (EU) from 2010 to 2021, by affiliation*. https://www.statista.com/statistics/746562/number-of-arrested-terror-suspects-in-the-european-union-eu

9 Statista (n.d.). *Terrorism in Europe - Statistics & facts*. https://www.statista.com/topics/3788/terrorism-in-europe/#topicOverview

10 Wikipedia (n.d.). *Killings and massacres during the 1948 Palestine War*. https://en.wikipedia.org/wiki/Killings_and_massacres_during_the_1948_Palestine_war

26 Fatwa

To many non-Muslims, the word *fatwa* is equated with "death sentence". The origin of this mistaken translation is usually the fatwa issued in 1989 by Ayatollah Ruhollah Khomeini of Iran in connection with the book *The Satanic Verses* by British author Salman Rushdie. The fatwa called on "all brave Muslims" to kill Rushdie and his publishers.

The Satanic Verses was purportedly a work of fiction. However, as Ziauddin Sardar[1] notes: "There is no vehicle more powerful for a direct onslaught on a people's cultural and religious identity than a work of fiction. It gives no recourse to the victims to shoot it down."

He compares the following dream sequence from *The Satanic Verses* to part of Martin Lings's well-known biography of Prophet Muhammad (pbuh) *Muhammad: His Life Based on the Earliest Sources.* This is from Rushdie:

> When the guardian of the temple … saw the approach of Khalid with a great host of warriors, he … went to the idol of the goddess … he hung his sword about her neck, saying, "If thou be truly a goddess, Uzza, defend thyself and thy servant against the coming of Mahound [a name used in the past to vilify Muhammad]." Then Khalid entered the temple, and when the goddess did not move the guardian said, "Now verily do I know that the God of Mahound is the true God, and this stone but a stone." Then Khalid broke the temple and the idol and returned to Mahound in his tent. And the Prophet asked, "What didst thou see?" Khalid spread his arms. "Nothing," said he. "Then thou hast not destroyed her," the Prophet cried. "Go again and complete thy work." So Khalid returned to the fallen temple, and there an enormous woman, all black but for her long scarlet tongue, came running at him, naked from head to foot, her black hair flowing to her ankles from her head. Nearing him, she halted, and recited in her terrible voice of sulphur and hellfire: "Have you heard of Lat, and Manat, and Uzza, the Third, the Other? They are the Exalted Birds …" But Khalid interrupted her, saying, "Uzza, those are the Devil's verses, and you the Devil's daughter, a creature not to be worshipped, but denied." So he drew his sword and cut her down.

Compare this work of fiction with the following factual account from Lings:

> The nearest to Mecca of the three most eminent shrines of paganism was the temple of al-Uzza at Nakhlah. The Prophet now sent Khalid to destroy this centre of idolatry. At the news of his approach the warden of the temple hung his sword on the statue of the goddess and called upon her to defend himself and slay Khalid or to become a monotheist. Khalid demolished the temple and its idols, and returned to Mecca. "Didst thou see nothing?" said the Prophet. "Nothing," said Khalid. "Then thou hast not destroyed her," said the Prophet. "Return and destroy her." So Khalid went again to Nakhlah, and out of the ruins of the temple there came a black woman, entirely naked, with long and wildly flowing hair. "My spine was seized with shivering," said Khalid afterwards. But he shouted, "Uzza, denial is for thee, not worship," and drawing his sword he cut her down.

A student submitting the first passage as an original piece of fiction would be penalized for plagiarism. It draws too heavily on the second, and is intended merely to ridicule.

Meaning of fatwa

In reality, a fatwa is an opinion issued by an Islamic scholar, on the basis of their knowledge of Islam, the Quran and hadiths, Arabic language, use of analogy (*qiyas*), consensus among scholars (*ijma*), different schools of thought (mathhabs), and other reliable sources. Only after lengthy consideration by an established scholar can a fatwa be issued, and it represents that scholar's personal opinion.

Fatwas are not binding, as they only represent opinions on contentious issues. Abu Hanifa, the founder of the Hanafi school of thought (mathhab), said: "This knowledge of ours is opinion; it is the best we have been able to achieve. He who is able to arrive at a different conclusion is entitled to his opinion as we are entitled to our own."

Nowadays, fatwas are issued on a number of topics relating to modern everyday life, and are intended to clarify the Islamic point of view on questionable subjects, in order to allow Muslims to lead peaceful lives according to the Quran and Sunnah. Fatwas thus mostly cover topics such as vaccination, women's rights, the wildlife trade, kidney donation, marriage, nuclear energy, and smoking. In short, they do not call for the execution of another human being.

Mufti

People in New Zealand are familiar with this word, from the practice of schools allowing their students not to wear school uniform on particular days. Usually, students who turn up in everyday clothes are expected to give a "gold coin donation" (i.e. $1 or $2), and the money collected is donated to a charity. A very popular practice with the students, and an admirable way of raising money for charity.

Mufti school days are found in several other countries including Australia, Bangladesh, Canada, Fiji, India, Ireland, Nigeria, Pakistan, the United Kingdom, and Zimbabwe.

When used in this way, the word is normally pronounced muff-ti. However, many people may not realize that the word has Arabic origins, where it is pronounced moof-ti. The Arabic word *mufti* is related to the Arabic word *fatwa*. A mufti is therefore a religious scholar who can issue fatwas.

So, how are the two meanings of *mufti* (for everyday clothes, and for the Muslim cleric) related?

Heretaunga College in Upper Hutt, and Trident High School in Whakatane, New Zealand, changed their "Mufti Day" in 2020[2]. Heretaunga are now calling it "Be Yourself Day", and Trident have adopted the Māori expression "Kakahu Kainga" meaning "home clothes". The schools decided to drop the word *mufti* after learning the origins from an article by the New Zealand online magazine and news site *The Spinoff*.

The article[3], by historian Katie Pickles, describes how the term was coined.

> Once upon a colonial time during the Raj in India, off-duty British military leaders adopted a subjugated culture's ceremonial clothing as their informal attire. It appears that officers started dressing in robes and slippers that they slightly mockingly thought resembled garments worn by Mufti. This happened at a time when, with the

> objective of rendering them obsolete and powerless, the authority of Mufti in India was being extinguished. From there, the British Army started using the word "mufti" for their days out of uniform when they wore loose and comfortable clothing (including dressing gowns). One culture's power dressing was another's play clothes.

So, the etymology of the word *mufti*, in the sense of everyday clothes, shows that it was used to ridicule the Islamic religion and its clerics.

1 Ziauddin Sardar (2004). *Desperately seeking Paradise: Journeys of a sceptical Muslim*. Granta Books.

2 Forsyth, K. (2021). Bay of Plenty school renames 'mufti' day due to cultural insensitivity. *Rotorua Daily Post*, 2 June 2021. https://www.nzherald.co.nz/rotorua-daily-post/news/bay-of-plenty-school-renames-mufti-day-due-to-cultural-insensitivity/O62BBHOHD2XDAW44PT5NYELW24/

3 Pickles, K. (2020). A mufti day is heaps of fun – but it's time to give it a new name. *The Spinoff*, 12 February 2020. https://thespinoff.co.nz/society/12-02-2020/a-mufti-day-is-enormous-fun-but-time-to-give-it-a-new-name/

27 Halal

If you look up the word *halal* in a dictionary or on the internet, you will probably find an explanation like the following: "Halal is an Arabic word meaning lawful or permitted. The opposite of halal is haram, which means unlawful or prohibited."[1]

Five categories

While this is true, it perhaps needs a little elaboration. Islamic law divides human activities into five categories:

1. *Wajib, fard* ("obligatory"): things that must be done, such as the five daily prayers, or fasting in Ramadan. In the Quran, God (Allah) specifies: "The prayer is obligatory for believers at specific times" (4:103). If you do these wajib things, you are rewarded, but if you do not, you are punished.

2. *Mustahab, mandub* ("recommended, encouraged"): things that are recommended, but not obligatory, such as extra prayers, forgiveness, and unselfish hospitality. In a hadith recorded in Muslim, Abu Said al-Khudri, a Companion, reported:

> Prophet Muhammad said: "Whoever has a spare mount should give it to one who has no mount. Whoever has spare provisions should give them to one without provision" and the Prophet mentioned so many kinds of wealth until we thought that none of us had the right to a surplus.

If you do these mustahab things, you are rewarded, but if you do not, you are not punished. These deeds are also sometimes called *sunnah*, meaning that they were the habit of Muhammad, but not actually obligatory.

3. *Mubah* ("silent, neutral"): things on which there is no clear guidance one way or the other, such as sleeping or eating (outside Ramadan). If you do or do not do these things, you are neither rewarded nor punished.

4. *Makruh* ("disliked, discouraged"): things that are disapproved of, but not actually prohibited, such as divorce. A hadith states: "The most hated thing before Allah is divorce" (Abu Daud). If you do not do these makruh things, you are rewarded, but if you do them, you are not punished.

5. *Haram* ("forbidden"): things you should never do, such as adultery, gambling, or *shirk*. In a hadith, Muhammad said: "Allah Almighty said: 'Whoever knows that I have power to forgive sins, I will forgive him and I will not mind, as long as he does not associate any partners with me'" (al-Mujam al-Kabir).

In other words, there is a mirror image of rewards and punishment.

So, while haram is the fifth category, this means that all the other four categories are halal, that is, permitted. However, they are permitted to varying degrees. Wajib activities, by virtue of being obligatory, must also be halal, permitted. Even makruh activities, while being discouraged or frowned upon, are nevertheless permitted, or halal.

Halal food

Like many other aspects of Islam, the concept of *halal* applies to all facets of life. Thus, for instance, a person's job and other sources of income may be described as halal, or not. However, probably the most common context in which the word is used is in relation to food (halal butchers, halal restaurants, etc.). There are various requirements and prohibitions regarding halal food, the most relevant ones of which are the following:

- Any pig products are forbidden (haram). This includes pork meat, pork ribs, pork sausages, ham, bacon, gammon, lard, and anything derived from pigs.
- Other meat, such as chicken, lamb, mutton, and beef, must be slaughtered by (i) remembering God by saying *Bismillah ir-rahman ir-rahim* and *Allahu akbar*, as instructed in the Quran (6:118): "So eat of that [meat] over which the Name of God was pronounced, if you indeed believe in His revelations"; and (ii) slitting the throat in order to cause the animal

minimal discomfort and drain the blood, which is the body's way of flushing impurities. In short, people who do not eat halal-slaughtered meat are probably eating a lot of (congealed) blood.

- Any animals that have died before being slaughtered are forbidden. Thus carrion (the carcasses of already dead animals), roadkill and other dead animals are impermissible.

These prohibitions are contained in more than one place in the Quran: "He has forbidden you carrion, and blood, and the flesh of swine, and what was dedicated to other than God" (2:173).

- Also an animal that has suffered a strange death, is forbidden. In the Quran (5:3), God says: "Prohibited for you are carrion, blood, the flesh of swine, and animals dedicated to other than God; also the flesh of animals strangled, killed violently, killed by a fall, gored to death, mangled by wild animals – except what you rescue, and animals sacrificed on altars; and the practice of drawing lots. For it is immoral."

- Any alcohol is forbidden, including beer, wine, and whisky, either as a drink or in cooking. In the Quran (5:90), God says: "O you who believe! Intoxicants, gambling, idolatry, and divination are abominations of Satan's doing. Avoid them, so that you may prosper." Notice that it says "intoxicants" without specifically mentioning alcohol. So, any substance that intoxicates, and leads one to forget God (including all drugs), is forbidden.

- Foods containing ingredients such as gelatin, enzymes, emulsifiers, and flavors are questionable (*mashbuh*), because the origin of these ingredients is not known and often not declared on the packaging. For instance, some cosmetics may contain pork derivatives. Gelatin is often made from pig skin or bone and therefore may not always be halal. Muslims must check labels and ensure that any products containing gelatin – such as sweets – are halal and lawful.

However, Islam is a considerate religion and does not impose on anyone a burden greater than they can bear. So, if no other food or drink is available, and one is in physical danger of death from starvation or thirst, haram foods and drink may become halal, but only under those circumstances. The verse from the Quran previously quoted continues: "But if anyone is compelled, without desiring or exceeding, he commits no sin. God is Forgiving and Merciful" (2:173).

"Desiring or exceeding" here means that you should only eat or drink as much of the haram food and drink in order to prevent death from starvation or thirst. You should not continue eating and drinking after this point. Frankly, in the modern world, there are very few situations where this would be necessary.

Scientific corroboration

Muslims follow these restrictions because God commands them to. They believe that the Quran is the verbatim word of God, that He created all mankind, and therefore He is in the best position to tell us what is good for us. It is like reading the manual of a car to find out what kind of fuel it takes.

Recent scientific research reinforces some of these choices. A World Cancer Research Fund report[2] linked the kind of food consumed to cancers, especially colorectal ones. In particular, researchers say people should stop eating processed meats, such as ham, bacon and salami. Similarly, a 2020 study[3] concluded that the risk of colorectal (bowel) cancer rose 20% with every slice of bacon people ate per day.

The World Health Organization[4] published a statement in *The Lancet Public Health*, that "when it comes to alcohol consumption, there is no safe amount that does not affect health." Heavy drinking, particularly over time, can lead to high blood pressure, alcoholic cardiomyopathy (enlarging and weakening of the heart), congestive heart failure and stroke. Heavy drinking also puts more fat into the circulation of the body. A study by 40 researchers, published in the *British Medical Journal* in 2011[5], found that alcohol consumption was responsible for 25 – 44% of upper aerodigestive tract cancer, 18 – 33% of liver cancer, 4 – 17% of colorectal cancer, and 5% of female breast cancer. They conclude:

In western Europe, an important proportion of cases of cancer can be attributable to alcohol consumption, especially consumption higher than the recommended upper limits. These data support current political efforts to reduce or to abstain from alcohol consumption to reduce the incidence of cancer.

1 Asma Jarad (2015). Halal and healthy on the go. *Islamic Food and Nutrition Council of America*, 30 September 2015. https://www.ifanca.org/halal

2 World Cancer Research Fund (n.d.). *Limit red meat and avoid processed meat.* https://www.wcrf-uk.org/cancer_prevention/recommendations/meat_and_cancer.php

3 Bradbury, K. E., Murphy, N. & Key, T. J. (2020). Diet and colorectal cancer in UK Biobank: a prospective study. *International Journal of Epidemiology*, 49(1), 246–258. https://academic.oup.com/ije/article/49/1/246/5470096?login=false#133824902

4 World Health Organization (2013). *No level of alcohol consumption is safe for our health.* https://www.who.int/europe/news/item/04-01-2023-no-level-of-alcohol-consumption-is-safe-for-our-health

5 Schütze, M. et al. (2011). Alcohol attributable burden of incidence of cancer in eight European countries based on results from prospective cohort study. *British Medical Journal 342.* https://www.bmj.com/content/342/bmj.d1584

28 Ibadah

Arabic definition

The word *ibadah* is commonly used to describe worship. The Arabic word is defined in the *Dictionary of Modern Written Arabic*[1] as:

- to serve, worship or adore;
- to render religious service, worship or adoration;
- to obey;
- to obey with humility or submissiveness;
- to be or become a slave or in a state of slavery;
- to do what is approved (by God);
- to serve or worship (a god);
- to adore, venerate (someone, a god or a human being);
- to idolize or deify (someone);
- to accept the impression of a thing;
- to submit, devote, serve, worship, adore, venerate;
- to imbibe and reflect the divine attributes or morals on one's own person

The Arabic word *ibadah* is regularly translated into English as *worship*. However, the noun *worship* is defined in the *Longman Dictionary of Contemporary English* as "the activity of praying or singing in a religious building in order to show respect and love for a god". The verb *to worship* is defined as to "to show respect and love for a god, especially by praying in a religious building". As we can see, the English definition only captures a small snippet of the full meaning of *ibadah*. It also limits it mostly to religious activities in a mosque, church, temple, etc. As with many Arabic Islamic words, an English translation fails to capture the full picture, and defines the word within a Christian environment.

Abd

The noun *abd* is related to *ibadah*, and is used in the Quran in many places and with different meanings, to describe:

- a slave or servant, in contrast to a free person
- a male slave or servant, in contrast to a female slave or maid
- humans, whether male or female
- one who purifies his *ibadah* to God by following His laws and commands

In the Quran (2:178), the word *abd* is used to mean "slave or servant" as opposed to a free person. God says: "O you who believe! Retaliation for the murdered is ordained upon you: the free for the free, the slave (*abd*) for the slave, the female for the female. But if he is forgiven by his kin, then grant any reasonable demand, and pay with good will".

In 26:22, God describes how the Pharaoh enslaved the Children of Israel: "Is that the favor you taunt me with, although you have enslaved (*abbadta*) the Children of Israel?"

In the Quran, the word *abd* is used to mean "male slave or servant" as opposed to a female:

> Do not marry idolatresses, unless they have believed. A believing maid is better than an idolatress, even if you like her. And do not marry idolaters, unless they have believed. A believing servant (*abd*) is better than an idolater, even if you like him (2:221).

"And wed the singles among you, and those who are fit among your servants (*ibadi*) and maids" (24:32).

Regular worship

As pointed out above, ibadah is not limited to prayer ceremonies in a religious building. Rather, just as the declaration of faith is the definition of a Muslim and underlies his every action, so all everyday actions can constitute ibadah.

In the Quran, God explains that this is the purpose of life: "I did not create the jinn and the humans except to worship (*abudun*) Me" (51:56). The Arabic word *ibadah* suggests showing the utmost humility and submissiveness out of an adoring respect and love for someone, and such an attitude of willing self-abasement cannot justly be adopted towards anyone except God.

This is expressed in the fifth verse of the first chapter (al-Fatihah), which states: “It is You we worship (*nabudu*).” There is only one being who can satisfy our needs and only one being that has the right to be worshiped, to whom everything belongs. The fifth verse teaches us not to worship anyone else except God alone, as no one else can satisfy our needs.

In his book *Al-Arbain fi Usul al-Deen*, al-Ghazali, the 11th-12th century CE Persian scholar, described other forms that worship can take:

- Reciting the Holy Quran
- Remembrance of God in all possible situations
- Earning one's livelihood in accordance with the regulations of the Shariah
- Fulfilling one's obligations towards one's companions and neighbors
- Persuading people to act righteously and dissuading them from what is reprehensible and forbidden
- Following the Sunnah

Acts of worship can thus be much more than the pillars, and can be everyday actions. In a famous hadith, Prophet Muhammad (pbuh) said: “Actions are according to intentions, and everyone will get what was intended” (Bukhari, Muslim). In other words, everyday actions can be acts of worship, if they are performed with the right intention, of worshiping God.

Abdul

All Muslim parents want their children to grow up to be good Muslims. To remind their sons of this, many sons are given a name beginning *abd* (“servant”) followed by one of the 99 names of God. These 99 names are found in the Quran and describe attributes of God. Many people believe that the 100th name is *Allah* itself.

Thus, a boy may be named Abdullah (Abdu Allah, “servant of God”), Abdul Rahman (“servant of the Merciful”), Abdul Malik (“servant of The Lord”), or Abdul Aziz (“servant of the Mighty”).

Relying on God

Not associating anyone with God in worship means that one should fear or depend on God alone. One's hope should not rest in anyone else other than God, and one should not consider obedience and submission or service to another as obligatory as the worship of God. Total humility in front of anyone and the acts of worship such as the bowing and prostration in salah are to be reserved only for God.

Guidance can only be given by God. In the sixth verse of Surat al-Fatihah, God instructs us to ask Him for guidance and support: "Guide us to the straight path." Elsewhere, He points out the reciprocal nature of worship: "O you who believe! If you support God, He will support you, and will strengthen your foothold" (47:7).

In the words of one writer[2], ibadah is like a 24/7 pharmacy, in that you can pray to God, and carry out other acts of worship, at any time of day or night, for help with your physical and psychological issues.

1 Wehr, H. (1979) *A dictionary of modern written Arabic.* Otto Harrassowitz Verlag

2 Muhsin Qara'ati (n.d.). *Worship (ibadah) and servitude (ubudiyyah).* https://www.al-islam.org/commentary-prayer-muhsin-qaraati/worship-ibadah-and-servitude-ubudiyyah

29 Kafir

In the Quran (64:2), God (Allah) says: "It is He who created you. Some of you are unbelievers (*kafirun*), and some of you are believers (*mumin*)." However, because of that theological categorization, the Arabic word for the people who do not believe in God, *kafir* (also spelled *kaffir* in English), has sometimes been misused as a word of insult or abuse.

A neutral word

Dr Ragheb El-Sergany[1] is an Egyptian (and thus native Arabic-speaking) Muslim preacher, surgeon and academic who is best known for his studies of Islamic history, and his founding and current supervision of IslamStory, a website that deals with studies of the history of Islam. As he explained in a blog in 2012, the true meaning of the word *kafir* (for the person) or *kufr* (for the concept) is different, and not necessarily an insult.

In Arabic, the word *kafir* means "a person who rejects or denies", and likewise *kufr* means the state of "concealing, denying, rejecting". It is important to note that *kufr* does not specifically mean rejecting Islam, or rejecting God, or rejecting the Quran, or rejecting Prophet Muhammad (pbuh). It can be used for rejecting anything (as can its English equivalent, *disbelieve, deny, reject*).

This is shown by the following verse from the Quran (2:256): "Whoever renounces evil (*yakfur bi altaghuti*) and believes in God has grasped the most trustworthy handle; which does not break." In the ayah, the word *kufr* (in the form *yakfur*) is used for disbelieving in *taghut*. *Taghut* means everything that is worshiped other than God. So, God states that Muslims have to be kafirs – of *taghut*. They have to reject belief in, and worship of, anything other than God. From the Islamic point of view, this is therefore a good thing, not a negative thing or insult.

This is very similar to the declaration of faith (*shahadah*) that defines a Muslim. The first half (*la ilaha illa allah*) is often translated as "There is nothing worthy of worship, apart from Allah." This implies that Muslims must reject (be *kafir*s of) the worship of anything other than God.

Care when using the word

In everyday use (including by some Muslims), the word *kafir* is often used as an insult or almost a curse, referring to someone who rejects Islam. However, "if *kafir* was an insulting word, Allah would not have used it for Muslims."[1]

The proper translation for the common Islamic use should therefore probably be *kafirs of Islam*, meaning "a subset of society who have read, understood and rejected the message of the Quran. Literally, 'covering up' mentally and physically the manifest truth which is believed in Islam to be uncovered in the Quran."[2]

A Bukhari hadith warns us of the potential dangers of using the word *kafir* about someone. "Whoever calls his Muslim brother a kafir, then if he is not a kafir, it bounces back to the one who said it." In other words, we need to be 100% sure before calling someone a kafir. Since the person in the hadith is called *his Muslim brother*, it is unlikely that he is a kafir. It is better to keep silent, or to discuss things with the person.

The consequence of falsely accusing someone of kufr is laid out even more strongly in the following Bukhari hadith: "Cursing a Muslim is like killing him, and whoever accuses a believer of kufr, it is like killing him."

Other non-Islamic uses

As we have seen, the word *kafir* is often used (wrongly from the Arabic point of view) as an insult for disbelievers. As extensions of this incorrect usage, it has also been used:

- "... in South Africa to refer to a black person. Now widely considered an offensive ethnic slur, it was formerly a neutral term for South African blacks. The word is derived from the Arabic term *kafir* (meaning 'disbeliever'), which originally had the meaning 'one without religion.'"[3] The *kaffir lily* plant, *kaffir corn* grain, and *kaffir boom* tree have the same South African origin.
- as *Kafiristan*, for "present-day Nuristan Province in Afghanistan and its surroundings ... normally taken to mean *land of the kafirs* in Persian language, where the name 'kafir' is

derived from the Arabic 'kaafer' literally meaning a person who refuses to accept a principle of any nature and figuratively as a person refusing to accept Islam as his faith."[4] The *kafir harp* musical instrument has the same origin.

- as *kaffir lime*, for a fruit native to Asia. However, "*The Oxford Companion to Food* recommends that the name *kaffir lime* be avoided in favor of *makrut lime* because *kaffir* is an offensive term in some cultures and has no good justification for being attached to this plant."[5]

1 El-Sergany, R. (2012). Islam divides mankind into believers and kafirs (misconception). *Islam Story*, 23 January 2012. https://islamstory.com/en/node/31958

2 Wikipedia (n.d.). *Kafir*. https://en.wikipedia.org/wiki/Kaffir

3 Wikipedia (n.d.). *Kaffir (racial term)*. https://en.wikipedia.org/wiki/Kaffir_ (racial_term)

4 Wikipedia (n.d.). *Kafiristan*. https://en.wikipedia.org/wiki/Kafiristan

5 Wikipedia (n.d.). *Kaffir lime*. https://en.wikipedia.org/wiki/Kaffir_lime

30 Haqq and sidq

The word *truth* occurs frequently in English translations of the Quran. For example, in 10:35, God (Allah) says:

> Say: "Can any of your partners guide to the truth?" Say: "God guides to the truth. Is He who guides to the truth more worthy of being followed, or he who does not guide, unless he himself is guided? What is the matter with you? How do you judge?"

The Arabic word that is translated as *truth* here is *haqq*. However, *truth* is perhaps not the best English word to use for Arabic *haqq*. There is another Arabic word *sidq*, which is well translated as *truth*. Arabic *haqq* has several senses and connotations, but none of them relate to telling the truth. So what is the difference between these two Arabic words, *haqq* and *sidq*?

It should be pointed out straightaway that the words have different opposite words (antonyms) in Arabic. The opposite of *haqq* is *batil*, thus "unreality", with other possible meanings such as "void, dud, delusory". The opposite of *sidq*, however, is *kathab*, thus "untruthful, lying".

Haqq

Haqq may more accurately be translated into English as *reality*. That is, it refers to things as they really are, things that actually exist. *Al-Haqq* is one of the 99 names of God in the Quran.

> Say: "Who provides for you from the heaven and the Earth? And who controls the hearing and the sight? And who produces the living from the dead, and produces the dead from the living? And who governs the Order?" They will say: "God." Say: "Will you not be careful?" Such is God, your Lord, al-Haqq (10:31-2).

In Sufism, *Al-Haqq* is often used to refer to God as the Ultimate Reality.

In the Quranic verse quoted at the beginning (10:35), the word in the original Arabic is *haqq*. The above verse may therefore be more accurately translated as, "Say: 'Can any of your partner-gods show the way to what is real?' Say: 'God shows the way to what is real.'" That is, God is real, He really created mankind, the Hereafter really exists, etc.

There are similar passages in the Quran (22:62), for instance: "That is because Allah is Al-Haqq, and that which they call upon other than Him is al-batil, and because Allah is the Most High, the Grand."

Also "And do not mix *haqq* with *batil* or conceal the *haqq* while you know [it]" (2:42).

The 69th chapter of the Quran is entitled *Al-Haqqah*. This is an emphatic form of *haqq*. It refers to the Day of Judgement, reminding readers that it is a reality that we will all face.

Sidq

Truthfulness (*sidq*) refers to whether what one says or writes about reality (*haqq*) is correct and accurate, or not.

A famous Bukhari hadith reports that Prophet Muhammad (pbuh) stood on Mount Safa and asked tribes of the Quraish:

> "Suppose I told you that there is an [enemy] cavalry in the valley intending to attack you, would you believe me?" They said: "Yes, for we have not found you telling anything other than the truth." He then said: "I am a warner to you in face of a terrific punishment [Hell]."

A narration in Tarikhi Tabari and Sirihi Halabiyih reports that Muhammad continued:

> "O people of the Quraish! I warn you to fear God's punishment. Save yourself from the fire. My position is the same as that of the sentry who sees the enemy from afar and warns his people of the danger of their enemies. Does such a person ever lie to his people?"

In this scenario, the reality (*haqq*) was that there was no army behind the mountain. If Muhammad had said that there was an army, he would have been lying. However, he was speaking hypothetically, in order to establish that he is a person that always tells the truth (*sidq*). He then went on to say that there is a severe torture (Hell, Jahannam). He was being truthful (*sidq*) about the reality (*haqq*) of Hell.

So, *sidq* relates to people saying or writing whatever corresponds to reality. They are giving a truthful (*sidq*) description of reality (*haqq*). They are not lying.

The difference in meaning between reality (and fact) and truth is one that is debated in philosophy. However, different philosophers may use the terms in different ways, with differing definitions and implications. An additional problem is that the imprecision of colloquial and idiomatic language may blur the distinction, such that the terms are used almost interchangeably. In English, we can say: "The dream became a reality" or "The dream came true" to describe the same situation.

Essentially, the terms belong to different fields. Truth relates to items in language, that is, the words used to describe entities and situations. Reality, on the other hand, relates to items in the world, that is, whether they exist or not. The dream became a reality because it did not exist in the world (it was only a dream or plan) and later it did exist in the world.

The English word *truth* comes originally from the Old English *trēowþ* which in turn comes from the Proto Indo-European *dru-* meaning "tree" derived from *deru* meaning "solid, firm". This implies that truth is something set, solid, unchangeable, withstanding all kinds of weather. The root meaning of the Arabic word *sidq* is similar to that of the Proto Indo-European *deru*, namely strength and hardness.

This strength is shown by the fact that telling the truth is required of all Muslims. Muslims who are truthful can hope for Paradise (Jannah), God willing, insha Allah.

In the Quran (5:119), God says:

> God will say, "This is a Day when the truthful [sidq] will benefit from their truthfulness [sidq]." They will have Gardens beneath which rivers flow, wherein they will remain forever. God is pleased with them, and they are pleased with Him. That is the great attainment.

In a hadith, Muhammad said:

> It is obligatory for you to tell the truth (sidq), for truth leads to

virtue and virtue leads to Paradise, and the man who continues to speak the truth and endeavors to tell the truth is eventually recorded as truthful with Allah. And beware of telling of a lie for telling of a lie leads to obscenity and obscenity leads to Hellfire, and the person who keeps telling lies and endeavors to tell a lie is recorded as a liar with Allah (Muslim).

The emphasis that is put on telling the truth in Islam is shown by many verses in the Quran:

"O you who believe! Be conscious of God, and be with the sincere (*sidq*) [in word and deed]" (9:119).

"And say, 'My Lord, lead me in through an entry of truth (*sidq*), and lead me out through an exit of truth (*sidq*), and grant me from You a supporting power'" (17:80).

"And give me a reputation of truth (*sidq*) among the others" (26:84).

"The righteous will be amidst gardens and rivers in an assembly of virtue (*sidq*), in the presence of an Omnipotent King" (54:54-5).

Many people are described as being truthful (*sidq*). Abu Bakr, who became the first leader of the Muslims (caliph) after the death of Muhammad, was called *As-Siddiq* by Muhammad, because his faith was too strong to be shaken by anything, and he thus always told the truth. *As-Siddiq* is thus a title, not a surname. Similarly, Abu Bakr's daughter and the Prophet's wife, Aishah, is also called *As-Siddiqah*.

Prophets are also described as truthful: "And mention in the Scripture Abraham (Ibrahim). He was a man of truth (*sidq*), a prophet" (19:41).

After reciting from the Quran, Muslims sometimes say: *Sadaqa Allah al-Athim* ("God the Almighty has spoken the truth"). There are differing opinions as to whether there is authority for this. Those who state that it is permissible quote as evidence the verse: "Say [O Muhammad]: 'God has spoken the truth (*sadaqa Allah*), so follow the religion of Abraham (Ibrahim) the Monotheist; he was not a Pagan'" (Quran 3:95). This means that God had spoken the truth in all that He had said to His slaves in the Taurat (Torah), the Injil (Gospel) and all other revealed books.

We thus have two Arabic words, *haqq* and *sidq*. They are both often translated into English as *truth*. However, the difference in meaning between the two is perhaps best remembered by translating *haqq* as *reality*, and *sidq* as *truthfulness*.

In Islam, there are six things that Muslims acknowledge the reality (*haqq*) of: God, His angels, His books, His prophets, the Day of Judgement, and predestination. These are known as the Articles of Faith.

Some of them require no blind faith. We can all experience the reality of the Quran, by taking it off our bookshelf, and reading and reflecting on it. Few people, whether Muslim or non-Muslim, doubt that Muhammad really existed. As Muslim preachers often state: "You may try to deny God, but you can't deny Muhammad."

Whether what one says or writes corresponds to reality (*haqq*) is a matter of truth (*sidq*). Dictionaries define *truth* as "that which is in accordance with fact or reality". Human beings have free will and can choose to say what corresponds with reality (they can be truthful) or not (they can lie).

5

Unsung Heroes of Islam

Unsung Heroes of Islam

There are various personages who are well-known to all Muslims: Prophet Muhammad (pbuh), members of his family (including Khadijah, Aishah, Fatimah, and Ali), his Companions (including Abu Bakr, Umar, and Uthman), those who opposed him (including Abu Sufian, and Hind). All of these characters played their part in the establishment of Islam in the late 6th and early 7th century CE. Any non-Muslim who has taken the trouble to learn a little about Islam will be familiar with some of them.

However, even Muslims may be hard put to name important Muslims in the 14 centuries since Prophet Muhammad's time. This is not for the lack of such people. There are many prominent religious scholars (e.g. Al-Ghazali), many important scientists (e.g. Al-Khwarizmi), and so on.

The fact that their names are less well-known is probably a result of how history books are written. The contribution of Muslims to science is often downplayed. While most people know of Omar Khayyam because of his poetry, notably the *Rubaiyat of Omar Khayyam*, his major historical influence on the fields of mathematics, astronomy and philosophy is seldom mentioned.

This section describes several lesser-known personages in the 14 centuries of Islamic history, from the Prophet's time (Bilal, Al-Arqam, Abu Hurairah) through subsequent centuries (Fatimah Al-Fihri, Ibn Sina, Lubna of Spain, Mansa Musa) to the present day (King Charles III, Sadio Mané).

It may seem incongruous that this list contains a non-Muslim (King Charles III). However, as Chapter 39 shows, he has a knowledgeable and very sympathetic outlook towards Islam.

31 Bilal

The story of Bilal ibn Rabah is inspirational, as it illustrates many of the virtues of Islam. Some details of Bilal's life are uncertain, and varying accounts exist. However, his conversion, his taqwa, and his position as the first caller to prayer (*muathin*) are not disputed.

Bilal was among the Muslims who migrated to Yathrib (later renamed Madinah). When the call to prayer (athan) was first given in Madinah, it was Bilal who was chosen to proclaim it. One reason for this was that he had a beautiful deep, melodious, resonant voice.

However, what is remarkable about the choice of Bilal is that he was a younger black African slave.

He was younger

The date of Bilal's birth is not known for certain, but historians put it at sometime between 578 and 582. This would make him about ten years younger than Prophet Muhammad (pbuh). That is, when the first muathin was chosen, it was not someone who was an elder, or had status and respect because of seniority.

He was black

William Muir in his book, *The Life of Muhammad*[1], states: "He was tall, dark, and with African features and bushy hair". He also states that noble members of the Quraish would despise Bilal and call him "ibn Sauda" ("son of the black woman"). In other words, racism based on skin color was rife even in those days.

He was of African heritage

Although Bilal was born in Makkah, he was the son of Rabah, an Arab slave while his mother, Hamamah, was a former princess of Abyssinia (present-day Ethiopia and Eritrea) who was captured after the event of Amul-Fil (the attempt to destroy the Kabah), and put into slavery. For this reason, Bilal is often referred to as Bilal al-Habashi, that is, "Bilal whose heritage is from Habesha" (another name for Abyssinia). In short, Bilal could hardly be called a true Makkan Arab.

He was a slave

He was born into slavery, and had no option but to work for his master, Umayya ibn Khalaf. As Aisha Stacey[2] states: "Being born into servitude, he probably never expected life to offer him more than hard work, pain and drudgery." Umayya's livelihood was based around idol worship; Bilal became recognized as a good slave and was entrusted with the keys to the idols of Arabia. He converted and was bought out of slavery by Abu Bakr, a Companion of Muhammad. The Muslims thus chose for their muathin not someone of high social standing, but a former slave.

The fact that a younger black African slave was selected to be given the honor of making the first call to prayer is testimony to Islam's pluralism and racial equality, and that in Islam people are judged by their piety (taqwa), rather than their age, skin color, race, ethnicity or social status.

The events of Bilal's history after the death of Muhammad are disputed. He migrated to Syria, where he died around the years 638 to 642. Given that his date of birth is not certain, this would have made him anywhere between 56 and 64 years old. The location of his tomb is not certain either. Most say it is Damascus (Syria), although others say Amman (Jordan).

Bilal's place in the history of Islam is assured for several reasons. He was one of the first converts to Islam. His allegiance to Islam was tested by torture, but he was steadfast in his piety. He was one of the closest companions of Muhammad. He was the first muathin. As a result of this, he is guaranteed Paradise (Jannah), because Muhammad called Bilal "a man of Paradise".

1 Muir, W. (1923). *The life of Mohammad from original sources*. J. Grant.

2 Stacey, A. (2011). *Bilal ibn Rabah: From slavery to freedom*. https://www.islamreligion.com/articles/4722/viewall

32 Al-Arqam

His full name was Al-Arqam ibn Abil-Arqam, a strange combination ("Al-Arqam, the son of the father of Al-Arqam"). His father was Abd-manaf ibn Asad ibn Umar ibn Makhzum, from the Makhzum clan of the Quraish tribe, and his mother was Umayma bint Al-Harith from the Khuza tribe. He was an early convert to Islam.

In the early days of the mission of Prophet Muhammad (pbuh), the Muslims were being harassed and persecuted by the Makkan Quraish, and it was unsafe for them to congregate. Al-Arqam's house was selected as a safe place to meet, pray and learn about Islam because it was located on the east of As-Safa Hill, where Muhammad was living.

As-Safa is the starting point for the Sai walk between it and Al-Marwah that is required of pilgrims performing Hajj or Umrah. This is in recognition of Hajar, the wife of Abraham (Ibrahim), who ran between the two hills in search of water for her baby Ishmael (Ismail). God (Allah) confirms this in the Quran (2:158): "Safa and Marwa are among the rites of God. Whoever makes the Pilgrimage to the House, or performs the Umrah, commits no error by circulating between them."

Al-Arqam's house was ideally situated, as it was in a narrow street and could be entered secretly. The entrance, and the street, could be observed from the house.

Among the early Muslims who came to the house and converted were two prominent members of the Quraish tribe: Muhammad's uncle Hamzah, famous as a warrior, and Umar, who became the second leader of the Muslims (caliph) after Muhammad's death (the first leader was Abu Bakr). At that time, the total Muslim community numbered only 40.

Al-Arqam's house (*Dar ul-Arqam* in Arabic) thus became the first Islamic school, with Muhammad as the teacher and the first Muslims as its students. The name Darul Arqam is thus closely connected with Islamic education, and is a commonly used name in Muslim circles, for converts' associations, dawah associations, Islamic schools, charities, Islamic media studios, etc., in places including Jakarta Indonesia, Singapore, Malaysia, Houston USA, Michigan USA, and Leicester UK.

Al-Arqam took part in the Hijrah migration to Madinah, where Muhammad granted him a house. He fought in many battles, including Badr, Uhud and the Battle of the Trench. He died in 675.

33 Abu Hurairah

The subject of this chapter is the great Companion Abu Hurairah. His name hardly goes unmentioned in Friday khutbahs, Islamic lectures, in the books of hadith, biographies of Muhammad (pbuh) (sirah), jurisprudence (fiqh), worship (ibadah) and religious gatherings, because his is the foremost name in the roll of hadith transmitters. As a result, many hadiths, in their chain of transmission, have him as the second-to-last link: "So-and so said that so-and-so said … that Abu Hurairah said that Muhammad said: …" Through his prodigious efforts, thousands of hadiths – at least 5,374 – were transmitted to later generations.

His real name was Abd Ar-Rahman ibn Sakhr. He was known as Abu Hurairah, "the kitten man", literally "the father of the kitten", because like Muhammad, he was fond of cats and since his childhood often had a cat to play with.

Abu Hurairah became a Muslim at the hands of At-Tufail ibn Amr, the chief of the Daws tribe to which he belonged. According to a Muslim hadith, he tried to convince his mother to convert, but she refused. He sought Muhammad's help.

> I have not let up in inviting my mother to Islam but she has always rebuffed me. Today, I invited her again and I heard words from her which I do not like. Do make supplication to God Almighty to make the heart of Abu Hurairah's mother incline to Islam.

Muhammad responded to Abu Hurairah's request and prayed for his mother. Abu Hurairah said:

> I went home and found the door closed. I heard the splashing of water and when I tried to enter, my mother said: "Stay where you are, O Abu Hurairah." And after putting on her clothes, she said: "Enter!" I entered and she said: "I testify that there is no god but Allah and I testify that Muhammad is His servant and His messenger."

Although he narrated many hadiths, he accompanied Muhammad for only four years. With his formidable memory, Abu Hurairah set out to memorize within just four years many sayings which could not be remembered by many other Companions who had much longer companionship with Muhammad.

At that time, he was not married. Unlike many of the migrants to Madinah (*muhajirin*) he did not busy himself in the marketplace, with buying and selling. Unlike many of the Madinan helpers (*ansar*), he had no land to cultivate or crops to look after. He stayed with Muhammad in Madinah and went with him on journeys and expeditions.

Many people were surprised by the number of hadiths that Abu Hurairah claimed to have memorized, and tested him. One, Marwan ibn al-Hakam, sat with Abu Hurairah and asked him to recount some hadiths. Unknown to Abu Hurairah, Marwan had a scribe behind a curtain, who wrote down what Abu Hurairah narrated. A year later, Marwan repeated the process, with the same hadiths. He found that Abu Hurairah had not forgotten a single word.

His father died when he was young, and he was often hungry and destitute. Busrah bint Ghazwan gave him food, and she eventually became his wife. When the Muslims were blessed with great wealth and material goodness, he became quite rich and was appointed governor of Madinah, and later of Bahrain. He passed away in the year 681 aged 78.

Muslims owe a debt of gratitude to Abu Hurairah for helping to preserve and transmit the valuable legacy of Muhammad.

34 Fatima Al-Fihri

The University of Oxford's first female Vice-Chancellor

In 2016, the University of Oxford appointed Professor Louise Richardson[1] Vice-Chancellor (equivalent to chief executive officer in corporate terms). She thus became the first female Vice-Chancellor in the university's nine centuries of existence. The exact date of founding of the university is not known for sure, but is thought to be around 1096. Her appointment came after 271 male Vice-Chancellors.

At the official installation, the Chancellor (ceremonial head) of the university, former Conservative Minister and Governor of Hong Kong, Lord Patten of Barnes, remarked: "I know that you would wish to be judged primarily not on the glass ceilings you have smashed, but on your achievements as an academic leader on both sides of the Atlantic." From 2009, Professor Richardson had been Principal (equivalent to Vice-Chancellor) of the University of St Andrews, the first woman to occupy the position. The fact that she was the first female CEO of two British universities was hailed as a triumph for women's liberation. She has since left the University of Oxford after her seven-year appointment, and joined the Carnegie Corporation of New York as its President.

Female academic leadership in the Islamic world

Let us contrast this with the Islamic world.

The Qarawiyyin mosque and religious school (madrasa) in Fez, Morocco was founded in 859. Today it is part of the University of Qarawiyyin, and the mosque is one of the largest in North Africa. It therefore predates the University of Oxford by over two centuries, and is recognized as the world's oldest university by UNESCO and Guinness World Records. Even this is disputed, as the Ez-Zitouna Mosque in Tunis, which hosted a university, was built in the early 8th century CE.

The Qarawiyyin mosque and madrasa was founded by a woman, Fatima bint Muhammad Al-Fihri Al-Quraish. Some aspects of her life are disputed. She was born around the year 800 in Al-Qayrawan in modern Tunisia. The city is nowadays known by its French spelling Kairouan, and is a UNESCO world heritage site. The family migrated to

Fez as part of a large migration from Al-Qayrawan. Her father became wealthy as a merchant and, on his death, this wealth was inherited by Fatima and her sister Mariam. To cater to the large number of Muslim immigrants to Fez, the Qarawiyyin Mosque was built, and Mariam sponsored the building of the Al-Andalus Mosque, also in Fez. Both the Qarawiyyin Mosque, named after the migrants to Fez from Al-Qayrawan, and the Al-Andalus Mosque, named after Muslim migrants from Spain, were part of a larger tradition of women founding mosques. Despite being founded by a woman, the Qarawiyyin madrasa did not admit women until the mid-20th century CE.

The Qarawiyyin Mosque took 18 years to build and was completed shortly before Fatima's death in about 880.

Another famous university that vies with the universities of Qarawiyyin and Ez-Zitouna as the world's oldest university is Al-Azhar University in Cairo, Egypt, which was established in 972, over a century before the University of Oxford.

So, in the Islamic world, there were universities at least a couple of centuries before the West, and female tertiary educational leaders nearly a millennium earlier.

1 Harker, S. (2016). First woman Vice Chancellor installed at Oxford. *The Oxford Student*, 17 January 2016. https://www.oxfordstudent.com/2016/01/17/69367

35 Ibn Sina

A scientific legacy

Islam has never had a problem reconciling the Quran with scientific discoveries. As explained in Section 2, the Quran contains many statements that are far above the rudimentary scientific knowledge of the time of Prophet Muhammad (pbuh), but which have proven to be true through recent research.

Starting in Muhammad's time (7th century CE), research by Muslim scientists created a Golden Age of scientific research and discoveries up to the 13th century CE. Much of modern science builds on the research and theories of earlier scientists. While readers will be familiar with former Western scientists such as Newton, Galileo and Copernicus, the contribution of Muslim scientists is often neglected.

Great Muslim scientists whose contributions should be lauded include Al-Hasan ibn Al-Haytham (optics), Muhammad ibn Musa Al-Khwarizmi (algebra), Omar Khayyam (geometry), Ali ibn Isa Al-Kahhal (ophthalmology), Abu Hanifa Ad-Dinawari (botany), Ismail Al-Jazari (robotics, mechanical engineering), Ibn Al-Nafis (pulmonary circulation of blood), Piri Reis (navigator, cartographer), Ibn Khaldun (social science), Ibn Al-Baitar (medicine), Thabit ibn Qurra (astronomy), Ammar ibn Ali Al-Mawsili (inventor of the hypodermic syringe), Al-Battani (astronomy), Abu Bakr Al-Razi (medicine), and Jabir ibn Hayyan (alchemy).

The list of medieval Muslim scientists is long, and covers all branches of science. Indeed, many scientists were experts in more than one field. A page in Wikipedia[1] lists over a hundred such Muslim scientists.

Ibn Sina's supernova observations

Ibn Sina (980 - 1037), also known in the West as Avicenna, was a Persian regarded as one of the most significant thinkers and writers of the Islamic Golden Age. He researched and wrote on philosophy, medicine, astronomy, alchemy, geography and geology, psychology, Islamic theology, logic, mathematics, physics, and poetry.

According to a story published on technology blog Gizmodo[2], a group of German scientists have discovered the supernova observations carried out by Ibn Sina. A supernova is the death of a star. It can collapse into a very dense neutron star or a black hole, or become a diffuse nebula. It has an enormous final explosion with the appearance of a new bright star that fades away over weeks or months.

German researchers Neuhauser, Ehrig-Eggert, and Kunitzsch translated a part of Ibn Sina's famous *The Book of Healing* (*Al-Kitab al-Shifa*). In the discovered portion of the book, Ibn Sina describes the widely documented SN 1006 supernova. His observation provides a new crucial observational point that the supernova was probably the brightest stellar event in recorded history, about 16 times as bright as Venus over a three-month period, so bright that it could be seen even during daylight.

In the description, Ibn Sina writes:

> It therefore happens that the burning and flaming stays for a (long) while, either in the form of a lock of hair or with a tail [i.e. in the form of a comet], mostly in the north, but sometimes also in the south, or in the form of a star among the stars [*kawkab min al-kawakib*] – like the one which appeared in the year 397 [Hijrah calendar, 1006 Gregorian calendar]. ... It remained for close to three months getting fainter and fainter until it disappeared; at the beginning it was towards a darkness and greenness, then it began to throw out sparks all the time, and then it became whiter and whiter, and then became fainter and disappeared. It can also have the form of a beard or of an animal with horns or of other figures.

SN 1006 was a supernova, widely observed from Earth beginning in the year 1006; at the time, the Earth was about 7,200 light years away from the supernova. First appearing between 30 April and 1 May 1006, it was also described by observers in China, Japan, Iraq, Egypt, and Europe.

1 Wikipedia (n.d.). *List of scientists in medieval Islamic world.* https://en.wikipedia.org/wiki/List_of_scientists_in_medieval_Islamic_world

2 Liptak A. (2016). Researchers discover ancient observations of a 1006 AD supernova. *Gizmodo*, 24 April 2014. https://gizmodo.com/researchers-discovered-new-observations-of-the-1006-ad-1772757463

36 Lubna of Spain

Hidden Figures

You may remember the film *Hidden Figures* from 2016. It tells the true story of black female mathematicians who worked at the National Aeronautics and Space Administration (NASA) during the Space Race of the 1960s. In particular, it follows the main character, Katherine Johnson, a brilliant black mathematician who calculated flight trajectories for Project Mercury and other missions. It also features NASA supervisor and mathematician Dorothy Vaughan, and NASA engineer Mary Jackson, both blacks. This was 1960s USA, where segregation between whites and blacks meant that, for instance, despite working alongside whites of whom she was their intellectual equal, Johnson had to walk several blocks in order to use a coloreds-only restroom. People welcomed the film, as it told what had otherwise been an untold part of the Space Race story, namely that many blacks were heavily involved in the US Space Race.

The milieu of Lubna

Parallels can be drawn with the story of Lubna of Spain. Also known as Lubna of Cordoba, she lived in 10th-century CE Cordoba, Spain, and died in 984. Details of her life and achievements are uncertain; some people ascribe this to the fact that she was a woman, and that she did not have a famous husband. The British writer and novelist Kamila Shamsie[1] suggests that some of the accounts ascribed to Lubna in fact relate to other women of the time, including one named Fatimah. Some of the details given below may therefore not be completely accurate.

> The land of Al-Andalus is famed for its beauty, olive groves and trees abundant with fruit. Al-Andalus currently forms a part of Southern Spain. The majority of the Iberian Peninsula was ruled and governed by Muslims for hundreds of years. Many of these Muslims came from Morocco as well as further afield from places

such as Baghdad and Damascus. Cordoba was one of the main cities in the Caliphate of Andalusia for many years. Built upon ancient Roman ruins, the city was far advanced in technology and resources compared to its European counterparts such as Paris and London. There was running water, street lights, bridges as well as scientific innovation and trendy fashion throughout Cordoba and Al-Andalus.[2]

Lubna's talents

Lubna was born a Spanish slave girl. However, she rose in her station in life until she worked in the royal court in Andalusia under the Umayyads. She was the personal palace secretary for Sultan Abd al-Rahman III (died 961) and his son Al-Hakam ibn Abdul Rahman (died 976) after him. She has been described as an expert in several fields: poet, copyist, scribe, royal library's acquisitions expert, private secretary, and mathematician.

Librarian

She became the Head of the Royal Library of Cordoba, which contained over half a million books. She also acquired more books for the library collection by traveling to cities of the Middle East including Cairo, Damascus, and Baghdad.

Copyist

She also added to the collection of the library by contributing works that she had transcribed herself, even translating many important historic Greek texts by authors including Euclid and Archimedes, that would have otherwise been lost to time.

Commentator

She was not only a writer and a translator, but also an annotator and commentator of the books she transcribed and/or translated, and other existing texts.

Linguist

The famous Andalusian scholar Ibn Bashkuwal (died 1183), who described the social and intellectual history of Al-Andalus, wrote: "She excelled in writing, grammar, and poetry."[3]

Mathematician

Ibn Bashkuwal also wrote that "her knowledge of mathematics was also immense and she was proficient in other sciences as well. There were none in the Umayyad palace as noble as her." [3]

It is said that she was so fond of mathematics that she walked the streets of Cordoba teaching multiplication tables and mathematical equations to the children who followed her, until they reached the palace walls beyond which access was restricted.

The story of Muslim women in the history of Islam must not be forgotten. However, as stated at the beginning, some of the details of Lubna's life and achievements are uncertain.

Various parallels can be drawn with the ladies of *Hidden Figures*. "The reason why so little is known about them says more about the dominant culture of historians and biographers who chose to omit these women from their accounts, than about the contemporaries of these women"[4].

While Katherine Johnson and Lubna may be best-known figures from these periods, they are not individual female geniuses. "According to Arab historians, in the time of Caliph Al-Hakam II, more than 170 literate women could be found in some suburbs of the city [Cordoba]; these women were responsible for making copies of valuable manuscripts"[5].

Similarly, when an IBM computer (that could replace human "computers") was installed in NASA, Dorothy Vaughan realized the implication and taught herself how to operate it, eventually bringing 30 of her black co-workers to the Programming Department.

However, while the ladies of *Hidden Figures* are discriminated against on the basis of their sex and their color, the absence of such discrimination has always been a feature of Islam.

1 Kamila Shamsie (2014). *The Islamic Golden Age: Lubna of Cordoba* (podcast). https://www.bbc.co.uk/sounds/play/b03vd5xt

2 Abdullah Hakim Quick (n.d.). *Muslim Spain's legacy.* https://muslimcentral.com/series/abdullah-hakim-quick-muslim-spain-legacy/

3 Khan, F. H., Farhat, N., Rahman, F. N. & Ansari, R. K. (2015). Comparative study of two cultures for female mathematicians. *International Journal of Engineering, Science and Mathematics, 4*(1). https://www.researchgate.net/publication/273004215_comparative_study_of_two_cultures_for_female_mathematicians

4 Frederique, P. (2015). *Forgotten women: Lubna of Cordoba.* https://almiraah.wordpress.com/2015/02/06/forgotten-women-lubna-of-cordoba/

5 Ali Al-Halawani (2017). A prominent Muslim woman: Lubna of Cordoba. *Truth Seeker*, 5 February 2017. www.truth-seeker.info/jewels-of-islam/prominent-muslim-woman-lubna-cordoba

37 Mansa Musa

The world's richest person

Mansa Musa is one of the most important people in history. *Mansa* in the Mande language of Mali means "ruler" or "king", and *Musa* is Arabic for Prophet Moses.

Some details of his life – especially precise dates – are sketchy. He was born around 1280 CE and ascended to power in the early 1300s under unclear circumstances. At its peak, Mali was the largest empire in West Africa. The Mali Empire at that time comprised modern-day Mali and parts of Guinea, Senegal, Mauritania, and The Gambia. The empire was the source for very pure gold and, as a result, the empire and its ruler were very wealthy. People estimate that, in modern currency, Mansa Musa was worth at least US$400 billion.

Rodulf Ware[1] of the University of California suggests that, in the medieval period, the only other empire that had similar military, economic and political strength to the Mali Empire was China.

Mansa Musa's Hajj

Mansa Musa is reported to have been a devout Muslim, and performed Hajj in 1324-5, a journey of 4,300 km. This involved overland travel via Cairo, and he took with him an enormous entourage. De Graft-Johnson[2] writes that he took:

- 60,000 men, all wearing brocade and Persian silk, including
  - 12,000 slaves, who each carried 1.8 kg of gold bars
  - heralds dressed in silks, who bore gold staffs, organized horses, and handled bags
- 80 camels which each carried 23 – 136 kg of gold dust
- maybe 18 tons of gold in total

He gave some of the gold to the poor along the route. It was reported that he built a mosque every Friday. Because of his nature of giving in Cairo, Makkah, Madinah and other places, Musa's massive spending and generous donations created a ten-year gold recession. Some critics say this was an ulterior motive for his journey – to increase the reputation of the Mali Empire. Perhaps it worked: the Mali Empire was visited by the famous Muslim explorer Ibn Battuta, during the reign of Musa's younger brother Sulaiman.

Philanthropic work

Returning from Hajj, Musa embarked on a program of cultural and scholarly development. He constructed the University of Sankoré in Timbuktu, and brought jurists, astronomers, and mathematicians from around Africa and the Middle East. The university had 25,000 students and one of the largest libraries in the world with roughly a million manuscripts. In the 1400s, there were 80 universities in the city of Timbuktu alone.

He built many other mosques and places of learning. He brought architects from Andalusia and Cairo to build his grand palace in Timbuktu and the great Djinguereber Mosque. Civilization flourished; Sergio Domian, a modern-day Italian scholar of art and architecture, wrote: "Thus was laid the foundation of an urban civilization. At the height of its power, Mali had at least 400 cities, and the interior of the Niger Delta was very densely populated." [3]

Musa died in about 1337 CE and was succeeded by his sons. The empire continued to flourish, but declined in the 15th century CE.

So, that is Mansa Musa, perhaps the wealthiest person in the history of the world. The fact that most readers have probably never heard of him says a lot about the Western historical tradition.

1 Ozynska, D. & Hartrick, A. (2021). The richest person who ever lived. *BBC News*, 12 April 2021. https://www.bbc.com/reel/video/p09dcbl0/the-richest-person-who-ever-lived?utm_source=taboola&utm_medium=exchange&tblci=GiBgL-h61omfgT7sy-9Z7ZgL1ljGdboKLygX8ljLrLk-Q9iCMjFQolMW3nN2QsqOtAQ (video)

2 de Graft-Johnson, J. C. (2015). Musa I of Mali. *Encyclopedia Britannica*. https://www.britannica.com/biography/Musa-I-of-Mali

3 LibreTexts (n.d.). *Mali*. https://human.libretexts.org/Courses/Lumen_Learning/Book%3A_Early_World_Civilizations_(Lumen)/Ch._11_African_Civilizations/12.7%3A_Mali

38 King Charles III

Queen Elizabeth II passed away on 8 September 2022. The next in line to the throne, Prince Charles, thus became king, known as King Charles III. The previous two King Charleses lived in the 17th century CE.

As the new British monarch, he is the head of the Church of England. However, this is a titular post, that is, an official position of leadership but possessing few, if any, actual powers. Over the years, he has shown interest in other religions, including Islam.

> In truth, the king is a devout Anglican [Church of England] whose deep engagement with Islam (as well as Judaism and Orthodox Christianity) is connected to his interest in Traditionalism, the esoteric 20th century school of thought whose early proponents railed against the modern world, believing that all the great religions share universal truths that could be antidotes to contemporary woes.[1]

Before coming to the throne, when he was the Prince of Wales, Charles's interest in Islam led to him becoming a Patron of the Oxford Centre for Islamic Studies. "Writer Robert Jobson in his book *Charles at Seventy: Thoughts, Hopes and Dreams*[2] noted that the monarch studies the Islamic holy book the Quran and signs letters to Muslim leaders in Arabic."[3] He once studied Arabic in order to better understand the Quran.

Royal quotes about Islam

What follows is a number of quotations from speeches delivered by King Charles about various aspects of Islam. They were all accessible and freely downloadable from his website when this article was originally written in October 2022. However, since his accession, the website has been revamped and the speeches taken down. Some can still be found, as speech texts or as videos, on the internet.

Muslims in Britain

The King acknowledges the contributions of Muslims to British society.

> I have already mentioned the size of our own Muslim communities who live throughout Britain, both in large towns like Bradford and in tiny communities in places as remote as Stornaway in Western Scotland. These people, ladies and gentlemen, are an asset to Britain. They contribute to all parts of our economy – to industry, the public services, the professions and the private sector. We find them as teachers, as doctors, as engineers and as scientists. They contribute to our economic well-being as a country, and add to the cultural richness of our nation.[4]

Western debt to Muslim civilization

He acknowledges that Islamic civilization flourished long before western civilization.

> If there is much misunderstanding in the West about the nature of Islam, there is also much ignorance about the debt our own culture and civilisation owe to the Islamic world. It is a failure which stems, I think, from the straitjacket of history which we have inherited.
>
> The medieval Islamic world, from Central Asia to the shores of the Atlantic, was a world where scholars and men of learning flourished. But because we have tended to see Islam as the enemy of the West, as an alien culture, society and system of belief, we have tended to ignore or erase its great relevance to our own history.[4]
>
> We need to remember that we in the West are in debt to the scholars of Islam, for it was thanks to them that during the Dark Ages in Europe the treasures of classical learning were kept alive.[5]
>
> Anyone who doubts the contribution of Islam and Muslims to the European Renaissance should, as an exercise, try to do some simple arithmetic using Roman numerals.
>
> Thank goodness for Arabic numerals and the concept of zero introduced into European thought by Muslim mathematicians![5]

Ignorance or discrimination?

Charles points out that, with increasing connectedness through technology, information about all topics, including Islam, can easily be found online and elsewhere.

> The depressing fact is that, despite the advances in technology and mass communication of the second half of the 20th century, despite mass travel, the intermingling of races, the ever-growing reduction – or so we believe – of the mysteries of our world, misunderstandings between Islam and the West continue. Indeed, they may be growing. As far as the West is concerned, this cannot be because of ignorance.[4]

Shared beliefs

Growing up as the son of the head of the Church of England, Charles obviously knows much about Christianity. His focus, however, is positively on the commonalities between religions, rather than negatively on their differences.

> It is odd, in many ways, that misunderstandings between Islam and the West should persist. For that which binds our two worlds together is so much more powerful than that which divides us. Muslims, Christians – and Jews – are all "peoples of the Book". Islam and Christianity share a common monotheistic vision: a belief in one divine God, in the transience of our earthly life, in our accountability for our actions, and in the assurance of life to come. We share many key values in common: respect for knowledge, for justice, compassion towards the poor and underprivileged, the importance of family life, respect for parents. "Honour thy father and thy mother" [the Bible, Exodus 20:12 and Deuteronomy 5:16] is a Quranic precept too. Our history has been closely bound up together.[4]

Extremism

In the West, extremism is often associated exclusively with Islam, even though people claiming to belong to other religions commit similar crimes. Charles warned people to guard against this bias.

> We must not be tempted to believe that extremism is in some way the hallmark and essence of the Muslim. Extremism is no more the monopoly of Islam than it is the monopoly of other religions, including Christianity. The vast majority of Muslims, though personally pious, are moderate in their politics. Theirs is the "religion of the middle way". The Prophet himself always disliked and feared extremism.[4]

Freedom of expression?

Two episodes in the last few decades have related to what some people call freedom of speech or freedom of expression. However, this does not lead to a carte blanche freedom to insult knowingly. In both cases, the authors knew well the hurt that they were causing.

The first episode was the publication in 1988 of Salman Rushdie's *The Satanic Verses.*

> In 2014, author Martin Amis told *Vanity Fair* that he had argued with Charles over his apparent refusal to support Salman Rushdie after a fatwa was issued against him following the publication of *The Satanic Verses.* Amis claimed that Charles told him that he would not offer support "if someone insults someone else's deepest convictions".[5]

The second episode is the publication in 2005 of cartoons depicting Prophet Muhammad (pbuh) by the Danish newspaper *Jyllands-Posten.* Prince Charles took the Muslim side, commenting:

> The true mark of a civilised society is the respect it pays to minorities and to strangers. The recent ghastly strife and anger over the Danish cartoons shows the danger that comes of our failure to listen and to respect what is precious and sacred to others.[4]

Conservation

Like his father, Prince Philip, Duke of Edinburgh, who passed away in 2021, King Charles shares a keen interest in all things to do with conservation and the environment. However, Charles related this to the teachings of Islam.

> From what I know of [Islam's] core teachings and commentaries, the important principle we must keep in mind is that there are limits to the abundance of nature. These are not arbitrary limits, they are the limits imposed by God and, as such, if my understanding of the Quran is correct, Muslims are commanded not to transgress them.
>
> The inconvenient truth is that we share this planet with the rest of creation for a very good reason – and that is, we cannot exist on our own without the intricately balanced web of life around us. Islam has always taught this and to ignore that lesson is to default on our contract with Creation.[5]

As a practical example of this, Charles designed the Islamic Carpet Garden for the 2001 Chelsea Flower Show and won a Silver-Gilt medal. The garden was then transported to his Gloucestershire home, Highgrove House. He described how it is inspired by Islamic traditions and plants mentioned in the Quran. "I planted fig, pomegranate and olive trees in the garden because of their mention in the Qur'an."[1]

Women's rights

Islam is often claimed to be a religion that discriminates against women, despite many passages in the Quran, and hadiths, that show the equality of women, the elevated status of mothers, etc.

> Remember, if you will, that Islamic countries like Turkey, Egypt and Syria gave women the vote as early as Europe did its women – and much earlier than in Switzerland! In those countries, women have long enjoyed equal pay, and the opportunity to play a full working role in their societies. The rights of Muslim women to property and inheritance, to some protection if divorced, and to the conducting of business, were rights prescribed by the Qur'an 1,400 years ago, even if they were not everywhere translated into practice. In Britain at least, some of these rights were novel, even to my grandmother's generation! Benazir Bhutto [of Pakistan] and Begum Khaleda Zia [of Bangladesh] became prime ministers in their own traditional societies when Britain had for the first time ever in its history elected a female prime minister [Margaret Thatcher]. That, I think, does not necessarily smack of a mediaeval society.[4]

Islamic finance

> King Charles realizes the morality of Islamic finance.
>
> It is surely a good idea to explore how the spirit inherent in the "moral economy" of Islam could enable a just and ethical approach towards the management of systemic risk in economics, in business and finance. The way risk-sharing, implicit in *musharaka*, works, for example, with lenders sharing the borrower's risk, and the notion of *mudharabah*, the sharing of profit. This is very different from the way that conventional finance transfers the risk quickly and frequently onto someone else with profit going just one way.
>
> I suspect that if the strict injunction of the Quran against *riba* were to be applied to the economic system that prevails at the moment, then the debt we have effectively incurred for future generations by the depletion of the Earth's natural capital would surely be found to be usurious and profoundly unacceptable. This is why financial and business organisations that keep to the principles embedded within Islam could be helpful in forging a more ethical approach that leads to equitable outcomes.[5]

Support for Muslims

As ordinary citizens, Muslims can sign petitions and letters of support for various Muslim causes. In his position, Prince Charles could not, but he could make his opinions known.

> According to Jobson, Charles believed that "marching in carrying a banner for western-style democracy was both foolhardy and futile". Charles has also told ministers that he no longer wishes to have his connections with Gulf leaders used for British arms companies to sell weapons. Then there's his sympathy towards the Palestinians, which may be why it was his son Prince William, and not Charles himself, who carried out the first royal visit to Israel in June 2018. It was only in 2020 that Charles made his first visit to Israel. He took care to visit the Occupied Palestinian Territories, where he declared it his "dearest wish that the future will bring freedom, justice and equality to all Palestinians."[1]

In addition to the King's speeches quoted above and referenced below, readers are encouraged to access other speeches by the King about Islam, some of which may be found on the internet.

1 Oborne, P. & Imran Mulla (2022). Charles III: How the new king became the most pro-Islam monarch in British history. *Middle East Eye*, 12 September 2022. https://www.middleeasteye.net/opinion/king-charles-most-pro-islam-monarch-british-history

2 Jobson, R. (2018). *Charles at seventy: Thoughts, hopes and dreams.* John Blake Publishing.

3 Al Jazeera (2022). King Charles: What are his views on Islam? *Al Jazeera*, 11 September 2022. https://www.aljazeera.com/news/2022/9/11/king-charles-what-are-his-views-on-islam

4 *A speech by HRH The Prince of Wales titled 'Islam and the West' at the Oxford Centre for Islamic Studies*, 27 October 1993. https://www.youtube.com/watch?v=1Y-hTS7Ccumc

5 Rayhan Uddin (2022). King Charles III: Five things the new British monarch said about Islam and Muslims. *Middle East Eye*, 13 September 2022. https://www.middleeasteye.net/news/king-charles-iii-five-things-islam-muslims

39 Sadio Mané

Sadio Mané is well-known as a footballer (soccer player in the USA, Australia and New Zealand) who has played for Metz (France), R B Salzburg (Austria), Southampton (England), Liverpool (England), Bayern Munich (Germany), and Al Nassr (Saudi Arabia). What is perhaps less well-known is that he is a Muslim and has carried out substantial charity work.

Rags to riches

He was born in Bambali, Senegal. It is a small village with a population of only 2,000. His father, who was an imam, was not keen on Sadio playing football, instead emphasizing education. However, his father died when he was seven, and he was brought up mostly by uncles, some of whom were also imams.

Sadio's heart was still in football, using grapefruits and stones for a football in his poor village where there were few real footballs. He was patently talented, and earned the nickname "Ballonbuwa", or "ball wizard".

At age 15, he ran away from home in secret to Dakar, the Senegalese capital, for a trial with a local team. He was found and brought back to Bambali, but negotiated with his family that he would concentrate on football at a Senegalese football academy.

Aged 19, he made his professional debut for Metz, and went from strength to strength, winning many accolades, as well as earning substantial salaries.

He is a devout Muslim. He has had to be careful to avoid Western habits, such as alcohol, pork and tattoos. When he was transferred to Bayern Munich, he was worried about the German culture of beer and (usually pork) sausages.

Charity work

> Before [my father] passed away, he had this kind of sickness for weeks. We brought him some traditional medicine and it kept him calm for three or four months. The sickness came back but this time

the medicine didn't work and because there was no hospital in Bambali they had to take him to the next village to see if they could save his life. But it was not the case.[1]

Being orphaned at such a young age, he said to himself: "Now I have to do my best to help my mother." He remembered that his sister had to be born at home because there was no hospital in the village. Now that he has succeeded at football, and become wealthy, he has not forgotten his promise to help his mother and others. In recent years, he has:

- donated £250,000 (US $314,000) to build a school in Bambali, and financed free laptops and internet for the school
- donated £41,000 (US $51,000) to the national committee fighting Covid in Senegal
- donated £500,000 (US $629,000) towards the construction of a hospital in Bambali
- financed the building of a petrol station and a post office for his local community
- donated €70 (US $75) per month to each family in Bambali (roughly equal to a month's minimum wage)
- donated 300 Liverpool shirts to residents of his village before the 2018 UEFA Champions League against Real Madrid. Liverpool lost 3-1, but Mané scored their goal.
- paid for 50 Senegalese fans to fly to Cameroon to watch their 2021 Africa Cup of Nations semi-final against Burkina Faso, which they won 3-1, with a goal from Mané
- donated 400,000 FCFA (francs of the Financial Community of Africa, about US $670) for the treatment of a boy injured in a traffic accident (Mané was admitted to the same hospital for a concussion during the 2021 Africa Cup of Nations)
- become an ambassador for Right to Play, an international non-profit organization providing equality and empowerment through sport and education to young girls and women in Senegal

In recognition of all this charity work outside football, Sadio won the inaugural Socrates Award presented at the 2022 Ballon d'Or ceremony. The accolade is named after the late footballer Socrates, who co-founded the Corinthians Democracy movement, in opposition to the ruling military government in 1980s Brazil.

Humility

In an Ibn Majah hadith, Prophet Muhammad (pbuh) states: "Every religion has a special character, and the characteristic of Islam is modesty." Mané exemplifies this, both on and off the football pitch[2]. He has said: "Why would I want 10 Ferraris, 20 diamond watches, or two planes? I built schools, a stadium, we provide clothes, shoes, food for people who are in extreme poverty. I prefer that my people receive a little of what life has given me." His humility is shown by the fact that, after Liverpool's 2-1 win against Leicester City in 2018 in which he scored, he was seen later that day helping to clean the restrooms in his local mosque in Liverpool.

1 Aarons, E. (2020). Sadio Mané: "I wanted to build a hospital to give people hope." *The Guardian*, 8 April. https://www.theguardian.com/football/2020/apr/08/sadio-mane-documentary-made-in-senegal-liverpool

2 Egerton, N. (2023). 11 times Sadio Mane proved he was the nicest man in the world. *PlanetFootball*, 10 April 2023. https://www.planetfootball.com/quick-reads/six-times-sadio-mane-was-the-nicest-man-in-the-world/

6

Conversion

Conversion

The topic of this final section is conversion to Islam.

Throughout this section, the word *conversion* is used, although there are two other terms that are often used for the same thing.

Muslims believe that all humans are born with a natural innate disposition (in Arabic, *fitrah*) to acknowledge the existence of a higher power, a God, and only one God. It is a classic example of nature versus nurture. Prophet Muhammad (pbuh) said: "Each child is born in a state of fitrah, but his parents make him a Jew or a Christian" (Bukhari, Muslim). As a result, Muslims view conversion from another religion to Islam as returning to a natural state of fitrah. For this reason, the word *revert* is sometimes used, rather than *convert*. However, as definitions and illustrative sentences in English dictionaries show, the English word *revert* often has negative connotations of returning to bad behavior.

- to return to doing, using, being, or referring to something, usually something bad or less satisfactory (Cambridge)
- *Jackson said her boss became increasingly depressed and reverted to smoking heavily* (Collins)

Another alternative term for convert is *new Muslim*. This is fine, provided the person has converted recently (although some might say that, because of fitrah, Islam is nothing new to them). It also raises the question of when a "new" Muslim becomes an "old" Muslim, or is simply welcomed into the worldwide Muslim community (*ummah*) as "a Muslim".

The first two chapters examine why born Muslims and converts embraced the religion. In many cases, it is because Islam gives their life purpose and structure; dissatisfaction with their previous religion, if any; and the aimlessness of modern life.

In his farewell sermon shortly before he died, Muhammad said: "All mankind is from Adam and Eve. An Arab has no superiority over a non-Arab, nor does a non-Arab have any superiority over an Arab; a white person has no superiority over a black person, nor does a black person have any superiority over a white person, except by piety and good action." Racism has no place in Islam.

To many non-Muslims, Islam is a very "uncool" religion, a relic from centuries gone by. However, as Chapter 43 shows, there are many modern musicians who have converted, especially in the jazz and hip-hop/rap genres – and you can't get much cooler than that. Many of these musicians are black and, along with the Hispanics in Chapter 42, this shows the color-blindness and lack of racism in Islam that appeals to many.

Being a universal religion, Islam has adherents from all walks of life. Converts to Islam are not just from the poorer, lower classes. In addition, roughly two-thirds of converts in many places are women. Both these facts are shown by the British career women in Chapter 44.

Throughout this book, we have seen the similarities between Christianity and Islam. And the most similar Christians are Unitarians and Christian Scientists, because they believe in the oneness of God (tauhid).

Finally, born Muslims are at an advantage and a disadvantage over converts. Having grown up in a Muslim environment, they probably know much more about Islam and Arabic than converts. However, it is sometimes difficult for them to separate Islamic culture from the ethnic culture they grew up in.

40 Why are you a Muslim?

In reference to being Muslim or not, there are three groups of people in the world: born Muslims, Muslim converts, and non-Muslims. This chapter addresses the first two groups, in order to help the third group.

To the question "Why are you a Muslim?", born Muslims might answer: "I am a Muslim because I was born a Muslim." This is hardly a satisfactory answer. People are born Muslims usually because their parents were Muslims, they were given Muslim names, and were brought up in a Muslim country or environment. However, *Muslim* is a religious term, not a racial term. At some point, probably in adolescence, they must have considered the religion they were born into and accepted it.

Muslim converts will find it easy to answer the question. They were, by definition, born, and probably brought up, in a non-Muslim environment and thus know something about another religion, or lack of religion. At some point, they were probably dissatisfied with this, explored other religions, and made a conscious decision to convert to Islam.

Vice versa, non-Muslims could be asked: "Why are you not a Muslim?" Often, the answer would be: "Because I don't know anything about Islam." Sometimes, a negative impression of Islam has been formed, largely through misrepresentation of Islam in traditional media (newspapers, magazines, television, and radio) and in social media. Islam is often described as the world's most misunderstood religion. As shown in Section 4, several Arabic/Islamic terms are regularly mistranslated.

The basics of Islam

The word which is the name of the religion, *Islam*, means "submission, obedience, surrender" to the will of God. It comes from the root form *s – l – m*, which also underlies *salam* ("peace") and *salama* ("wellbeing"). Thus, Muslims find peace and wellbeing by obeying God's instructions (see Chapter 25).

In English, a *teacher* is someone who teaches. In other words, the *-er* suffix means "someone who does this". Similarly, in Arabic, someone who submits to the will of God (Islam) is a "Mu-Islam" or *Muslim*. The *mu-* prefix likewise indicates "someone who does this", in this case "someone who submits to God".

In a nutshell, here are some of the basic facts of Islam:

- You have a choice to follow any religion, or no religion. You have the free will to choose, but you will be ultimately held accountable for your choice, and the decisions and actions that follow from it.

- Islam came from the first man on Earth (Adam) and was spread through a series of prophets, including Abraham (Ibrahim), Moses (Musa), Jesus (Isa), and the final messenger, Muhammad (pbuh).

- Muslims believe that all prophets conveyed the same message, namely that there is no deity worthy of worship other than God (Allah). In the Quran (21:25), God confirms: "We never sent a messenger before you without inspiring him that: 'There is no god but I, so worship Me.'" God lists some of the previous prophets:

  > Say: "We believe in God; and in what was revealed to us; and in what was revealed to Abraham, and Ishmael, and Isaac, and Jacob, and the Patriarchs; and in what was given to Moses and Jesus; and in what was given to the prophets – from their Lord. We make no distinction between any of them, and to Him we surrender" (2:136).

- Islam preaches that body and soul are related. The physical body has a defined period of life on this Earth, while the soul never dies. It continues its journey even after our physical death on Earth.

The function of Islam

We return to the original question: "Why Islam?" The answer is that it fulfills two functions: it gives our life (i) purpose and (ii) structure.

Purpose in life

"What is the purpose of life?" "Why are we in this world?" and "What happens when we die?" are age-old questions that people have asked themselves, and sought answers for. They are questions that all religions (and atheists) must address. A quotation attributed to the US writer Mark Twain (but perhaps coming from someone else), who was a skeptical Presbyterian, is: "The two most important days in your life are the day you are born, and the day you find out why." In other words, your life started the day you were born, and a question you should be asking yourself during your life is "Why was I born?"

Some people's purpose of life seems to be to become wealthy. But is that really a purpose in life? What if you achieve this goal? What then becomes your purpose? That means you have no purpose left in life after that. Even if you win the rat race, you are still a rat.

Many billionaires have found out that you can have too much money, far more than you need, and have given wealth away to philanthropic causes. Well-known examples include Warren Buffet (investor, donated US $42.8 billion), Bill Gates (Microsoft, $29.8 billion), George Soros (hedge fund manager, $16.8 billion), Michael Bloomberg (businessman, former Mayor of New York City, $11.1 billion), Mark Zuckerberg (Facebook, $2.7 billion), Michael Dell (computers, $2.25 billion), Ted Turner (CNN, $1.3 billion)[1]. As the proverb states: "You can't take it with you." A hadith of Muhammad about a dead person corroborates this: "His family, his wealth, and his deeds follow him. His family and wealth return, but his deeds remain" (Bukhari, Muslim).

People have different aspirations at different stages of life, and wealth is not necessarily one of them. A child of six would probably prefer a new toy to a check of a million dollars. A teenager would possibly choose to have a party with friends, food, or movies, over having a million dollars. An old man in his 80s would prefer good health to having a million dollars in the bank. Therefore we can see that amassing wealth cannot be the ultimate purpose in life.

Islam teaches us the purpose of life. God says in the Quran that the only purpose for which He created mankind is so that they would worship Him. "I did not create the jinn and the humans except to worship Me. I need no livelihood from them, nor do I need them to feed Me" (51:56).

Islam teaches us that worship is not limited to prayers or even the five pillars (see Chapter 28). In fact, worship includes all acts of obedience to God. For example, a person's going to work with the intention of feeding his family is considered worship (*ibadah*). Likewise, visiting a sick person with the intention of following the Sunnah (by saying prayers for their recovery) is also worship. Helping the poor and needy is also worship.

A further question was: "What happens after we die?" Islam teaches us that the life in this world is a test and a trial. We are put in different situations and are assessed on how we respond to them. For example, God might test us with a lot of wealth, or with serious sickness, to see if we remember Him and whether we spend our wealth in His way or on the path of Satan (Shaitan). God continues to give us free will in this world for as long as we live, the caveat being that we will be held accountable after our death for the decisions and actions we chose.

The first stage after our death is the time we spend in the grave (*kabr*). This place will be a place of happiness or torment, depending on the actions we took in our worldly life. We will abide in the grave until the Day of Judgement.

The second stage is the Day of Judgement. Every single human being to live on the Earth will face this day, whether they like it or not. On that day, we will be given our results and our final destiny – Paradise (Jannah) or Hell (Jahannam). If our scales are heavy with good deeds, and we have believed in God, we will, God willing, insha Allah, be given a place in Paradise. On the other hand, if we did not believe in God or our bad deeds outweigh our good ones, then we will be given a place in Hell.

We will not be questioned on any actions of other people, or their beliefs, or anything that we were unaware of or incapable of doing. God will be the sole judge. He will act fairly and justly, as there is no better judge than the Creator Himself. Fortunately, among the 99 names of God are *Rahman* and *Rahim*, both expressing extreme mercy, and there is no *Wrathful*. His mercy transcends His wrath, and He will have the final say.

Structure in life

Many people go through their life rather aimlessly. They know they need to go to work, perhaps Monday to Friday 9 – 5, but beyond that, there is little orderliness to their daily life. In contrast, Muslims follow what they believe to be a God-given order to their lives. Each day, they perform five prayers at specific times, and their other everyday activities are arranged around these. On Fridays, male Muslims go for Friday congregational prayers rather than having a long Friday lunch. Once a year, in the ninth lunar month of Ramadan, Muslims fast from dawn to sunset (see Chapter 9), which instills order and discipline in their lives. Muslims are required, if able, to go on Hajj once in their lifetimes, a pilgrimage that requires planning for dates, for cover of work duties, and financial planning, as well as mental preparedness.

In all the above ways, Muslims avoid the aimlessness that comes with not knowing the purpose of life, and they structure their lives in order to complete the directives of God.

In summary, for the disbeliever, the purpose of life may be to amass wealth, money, power, fame, or position. Some of this may involve shady business practices. As we have seen, many billionaires realize they have far more money than they need. For some people, a sizeable part of their lives consists of excessive drinking, eating, drugs and gambling. Again, none of this will help them after they die.

Islam has answers to the important questions in life. Islam thus gives purpose and structure to life. The purpose of life can be summarized in just two words: Obey God.

1 Forbes (2021). The 25 most philanthropic billionaires. *Forbes*, 19 January 2021. https://www.forbes.com/sites/forbeswealthteam/2021/01/19/americas-top-givers-the-25-most-philanthropic-billionaires/?sh=51dae1231f59

41 Why people convert

There are numerous books on the market with titles such as *Why I embraced Islam, My journey to Islam,* and *I became a Muslim*[1], all giving details of the conversion process that people went through in discovering and accepting Islam. They all have a different story to tell, but there are also common threads that many of them share.

The stories are different because they are different people, were born into different circumstances, have different personalities, and have years of different experiences. Nevertheless, the common threads relate to reactions to, and disillusion with, the circumstances into which they were born, encounters with Islam and Muslims, and final acknowledgment that Islam represents what they believe and want to follow for the rest of their lives.

Family background

What religious circumstances are converts born into? The largest world religion is Christianity, so it is not surprising that a large number of converts to Islam come from that religion. A large number of the testimonies in books of conversion stories, because they are written in English, are from the USA and UK. A common theme is for writers to say that they were born into a Christian environment, but it was only a nominally Christian environment. That is, the family were not practicing Christians and only went to church rarely, if at all. At the other extreme, some had fathers who were pastors.

Especially in stories from the USA, in particular rural areas, writers say that the environment was mono-religious, that is, there were no Muslims, Buddhists, Hindus, etc. in the neighborhood. At best, people knew some Jews but, as Judaism shares much with Christianity, such as prophets including Adam, Noah, Abraham, David, Solomon (Adam, Nuh, Ibrahim, Daud, Sulaiman), that hardly led people to question matters.

As a result of this mono-religious environment, there was widespread ignorance about other religions, including Islam, because people never met Muslims, Buddhists, Hindus, etc. Religious classes at school focused overwhelmingly on Christianity, perhaps with a little Judaism, and the barest minimum about other religions, often only to point out why they are wrong.

One factor on which many writers agree, however, is disappointment with Christmas at a young age. In the West, Christmas is largely a non-religious celebration (celebration of what?) with plenty of recent innovations. A common comment is that so much seemed to be focused on Santa Claus (called Father Christmas in the UK) rather than Jesus (Isa), and on food, drinking, and children receiving presents. Could Santa Claus really travel around the world on Christmas Eve night, in a flying sleigh with reindeer, dropping presents into chimneys – even in those houses that had no chimneys? Eventually, often around the age of eight, children work out for themselves that it is illogical and untrue, or are told it is not true by older siblings, or stay awake on Christmas Eve night to witness Mommy and Daddy depositing presents. The disappointment that Mommy and Daddy have been lying to them leads to wondering whether what Mommy and Daddy say about Christianity and Jesus is also true or not.

Questioning

Disappointment about Christmas often leads to questioning about other aspects of Christian belief, especially the central concept that Jesus was the literal son of God and died on the cross for the sins of mankind (known in Christianity as atonement). (None of this corresponds to Muslim belief about Jesus.) Typically in teenage years, or early 20s, people start asking questions to their pastor, their family, and their Christian friends. However, a common remark in testimonies is that they never felt that they received a satisfactory answer. They were often told to "have faith". This, however, was felt to be the opposite process to reason: you should believe in something because it makes sense, not have faith so that something makes sense without further questioning.

Many writers, having grown up in Christian environments, state that they always believed that there is a greater power, a higher being, a God, but could never accept the concept that Jesus was the literal son of God. They also comment that Christianity seemed to focus exclusively on Jesus, almost at the expense of any focus on God (the Father, in Christian terms). Also, the concept of atonement, Jesus dying for the sins of mankind, and mankind being saved (salvation) by this, ran counter to the concept of free will, freedom of choice of action, and personal responsibility for your choices and actions.

Many writers, at this stage, started reading the Bible more closely than previously. Indeed, many felt that there had been selective coverage by pastors, and that the whole of the Bible had not been covered. As a result, they began to find rules in the Bible that did not seem to be followed by Christians. As one writer expressed it, Christians seemed to be adapting the religion to suit their personal preference.

Some said they started attending church more regularly than they had, in order to gain answers, but only found a lot of singing and, in some churches, guitar-playing.

Encountering Islam

At this age (teenage and early 20s), most writers started encountering Islam, and discovering what they had never known. There are two main pathways here: encountering Muslims, who informed them about the religion and also exhibited Islam in their daily lives; and reading extensively.

Encountering Muslims

There are three main ways in which non-Muslims met Muslims and thus Islam. Firstly, many writers went to college, university, or work, and had Muslim classmates and workmates. Secondly, some happened to have Muslims who moved into their neighborhood. Thirdly, a few traveled to Muslim countries.

However, all the above are merely ways of encountering Muslims; they do not necessarily lead to interest in the religion. This is where *dawah* ("invitation" or "calling people to Islam") comes in, and there are two forms.

Firstly, the Muslims may talk to the non-Muslims explicitly about Islam. In many cases, the non-Muslims were delighted to hear that God (Allah) is central to Islam and that Jesus is highly respected as a human prophet of God (and not the literal son of God), as that often corresponded to what they already believed.

Secondly, the non-Muslims were impressed by the character and conduct of the Muslims. The Muslims are often described as being respectful and contented, with an inner peace.

Reading about Islam

Some writers took a more intellectual approach, often exploring all major world religions. They thus re-read the Bible, and read the scriptures of Buddhism, Hinduism, etc., and ultimately the Quran.

They had often been told that the Quran was not worth reading as it was the work of Satan. However, on reading the Quran, about which they usually knew nothing, they were surprised that, instead of a sinister, strange, foreign, exotic book that they could quickly discount, it was full of what they were already familiar with from the Bible: stories of the prophets mentioned in the Bible. In addition, many writers said that they were overwhelmed by the power of the Quran, even though they read it in English translation, as it spoke directly to them, with guidance, arguments and counterarguments.

This directness is the result of a grammatical phenomenon about the Quran. Scriptures that relate stories are in the 3rd person (see Chapter 3). In contrast, many parts of the Quran are in 1st and 2nd person. That is, God, as the author of the Quran, refers to Himself as *I* or *We*, and He addresses various readers as *you*, *O believers*, or *O mankind*. In the Quran, God speaks directly to whoever is reading it.

Some writers were also convinced by books such as Maurice Bucaille's 1976 book *The Bible, The Quran and Science*[2]. Christians have always been uneasy about the inconsistency between what the Bible says and what has been discovered by modern science. As Bucaille's book details, there are many Quranic descriptions of scientific phenomena that would have been meaningless to Arabs in the 7th century CE, but have since been shown to be accurate (see Section 2).

Taking the plunge

At what point do you stop talking to Muslims and reading about Islam and the Quran, as an intellectual exercise, and decide that Islam is the religion for you – that is, convert?

At one extreme, some people convert almost immediately, even after reading just a few verses or chapters of the Quran. It corresponds so exactly to what they have been searching for, that they feel ready to convert. This may not be a wise move, however, as Islam is often described as being not so much a religion, that is, something you practice on one or two days per week, but a way of life, that is, something that is omnipresent and constant, and affects all aspects of your life. You need to be fully aware that, on conversion, you should start praying five times a day, only eat halal food, fast during Ramadan, give zakah, etc. These may not be minor changes in lifestyle.

At the other extreme, most people convert at a much more gradual pace. They may start by trying Muslim prayers. They may think that it does not make sense to convert to Islam if you have not read the Quran, its holy book (and it is not a short book, and needs understanding and contemplation). They may try fasting in Ramadan (and usually find out that it is not difficult at all). And so on. Eventually, they may think, or someone may ask them: "In what way are you not a Muslim?" They already believe in God and Prophet Muhammad (pbuh) and are already performing the practices; there is nothing important left.

This is, of course, not to say that once you convert, you know everything about Islam and do not need to continue learning. To convert, you only need to say, with 100% conviction, that nothing is worthy of worship except God and Muhammad is His final messenger. Other, more advanced aspects, such as learning Arabic, reading the hadiths, or planning to go on Hajj can wait. Being a Muslim and learning Islam is truly lifelong learning.

Helping those interested in Islam

All the above is simply a summary of common threads contained in first-hand conversion stories. If that is the way that many people come to Islam, what does that tell Muslims about how they should perform dawah?

An important point is that every Muslim is a *dai* (someone who performs dawah). Some dawah is deliberate (sitting down and talking to someone about Islam), while it can be unintentional (simply displaying everyday Islamic behavior, that people may be impressed by).

As many stories tell, much dawah is the result of non-Muslims simply meeting Muslims and realizing that, rather than the sinister, evil people they have been told to expect, they are in fact pleasant and kind. It is not so much the result of non-Muslims attending dawah classes, and other religious talks and sessions.

As much dawah is dawah by example, it is important that Muslims display good manners, behavior and conduct (*akhlaq*).

It is also important that Muslims are welcoming of new or potential converts. Some stories tell of people who showed an interest in Islam or even in converting, but when they went to the mosque, they were met by unfriendly Muslims who gave them the cold shoulder, sometimes because of nationality and heritage issues. The non-Muslim felt lonely and unwelcome, and in some cases they might have not converted, except for strong conviction that Islam is the truth.

A similar problem is "after sales service", that is, support for the new convert. The issue is the reaction of their family and friends. In some cases, there is no problem as the family and friends are not particularly religious and are happy that the convert is happy. However, in many cases, the convert is rejected by the family and/or friends, even to the extent of being told that they will rot in Hell. Support from Muslims is essential here.

Some dawah is dawah by teaching, so it is important that Muslims correct any misconceptions that non-Muslims may have, or untruths that they have read or heard in the media. They should also be persuaded to only read literature about Islam written by Muslims, as literature written by non-Muslims is usually inaccurate and biased. Even better, give them Muslim literature that is at the right level, in terms of their knowledge about Islam and their age.

Converting to Islam is not something that should be taken lightly, as Islam is a way of life, and therefore conversion is a life-changing experience. Dawah should proceed at the pace that the person can handle. The important thing is that they should not convert unless they are 100% certain. This certainty is something that converts often mention in testimonies, and they welcomed. If they reach certainty quickly, that is fine. However, most people take time, perhaps a couple of years or more. And that is fine too.

1 For example:

Backer, K. (2012). *From MTV to Mecca: How Islam inspired my life.* Arcadia Books and Awakening Publications.

Booth, L. (2018). *Finding peace in the Holy Land: A British Muslim memoir.* Kube Publishing.

Ismaiza Ismail (2005). *Why I embraced Islam.* Perniagaan Jahabersa, Malaysia.

Muhammad Haneef Shahid (2002). *Why women are accepting Islam.* Darussalam.

My path to Islam: Australian Muslim revert stories (2004). Islam-Australia and Goodword Media.

Parry, A. (2012). *I became A Muslim.* International Islamic Publishing House.

Priests embracing Islam (n.d.). https://islammessage.org/en/book/99/Priests-Embracing-Islam

Stories of new Muslims (n.d.). https://www.muslim-library.com/dl/books/English_Stories_of_New_Muslims.pdf

2 Bucaille, M. (1976). La Bible, le Coran et la Science: Les Écritures Saintes examinées à la lumière des connaissances modernes (The Bible, the Quran, and Science: Holy Scriptures examined in the light of modern knowledge). Publishers Seghers. https://ia601805.us.archive.org/11/items/the-bible-the-quran-and-science_202012/The%20Bible%20The%20Quran%20and%20Science.pdf

42 US Hispanic conversions

The term *Hispanic* refers to people who speak Spanish and/or are descended from Spanish-speaking populations. In the USA, it is similar to, and often used indistinguishably from, the term *Latino* which more strictly refers to those who are from, or descended from people from, Latin America, regardless of their proficiency in Spanish. Latin America is taken to comprise Mexico, most of Central and South America, and in the Caribbean, Cuba, the Dominican Republic, Haiti, and Puerto Rico.

Statistics

The United States Census Bureau does not provide statistics on religion. It is therefore left to other bodies to collect such data. Reported figures may thus not be totally accurate.

In 2009, only 1% of US Muslims identified as Hispanic, but by 2018, this had risen to 7%, according to a report by the Washington D.C.-based Institute for Social Policy and Understanding. As the institute's director of research, Dalia Mogahed, observed: "That's a 700 percent growth in less than 10 years, and no other group has grown at this rate."[1] This upsurge is partly due to conversions, but also to a high birth rate.

In 2018, only 1% of US Hispanics were Muslims, 55% being Catholics and 20% Protestants, according to Pew Research Center reports[2]. However, these US Muslim Hispanics represent 20% of all US Muslims.

Other estimates of the size of the US Latino Muslim population, and their nature, are contained in Claremont McKenna College, Green, Martin, and Mogahed, Kiramullah & Chouhoud[3]. The figure is well over 200,000.

Martin (2006) reported that the majority of Latinos converting to Islam were in fact Latinas, i.e. women.

Houston Spanish Islamic center

In order to cater to the needs of these Spanish-speaking Muslims, the Centro Islamico mosque was established in Houston, Texas in 2016 by Islam in Spanish, which was founded 15 years earlier. Islam in Spanish was originally set up in order to produce Spanish language versions of Islamic materials and the Quran. It started by producing more than 500 audio books and 250 videos, many of which were aired on public access television. It has since concentrated on internet materials and reaches audiences in Brazil, Argentina, Spain, Germany and France. In its first months, the center had 28 Hispanic converts. Alex Gutierrez, the center's development and operations director, estimates around 1,000 Hispanic Muslims live in the Houston area.

Reasons for conversion

Why do Hispanics, most of whom have a Catholic background, find Islam so appealing? There are many reasons[1].

The power of the Quran is often an important factor in a person's conversion. Maria Dawood borrowed a friend's Spanish translation of the Quran. "I couldn't stop. I continued reading. Once I finished, I started again. Every time I read it, I found something new. This is what I had been looking for."

Most of the prophets of Islam mentioned in the Quran are also prophets of Christianity mentioned in the Bible. Convert Imam Isa Parada explained: "Most Latinos think Muslims don't believe in Jesus and Mary. That gave them a different perspective of Islam."

Disillusionment with Christianity, and the closeness of Islam to Christianity, also play an important part. Nahela Morales relates: "As far back as I can remember, I was always looking for God," but her questions about Christianity were not answered and she was told to "always believe". "By my mid-20s, that wasn't good enough." She investigated various religions and finally read the Quran.

> When I came across Islam, I was encouraged to ask questions. All my questions were answered. I got a Bible to compare with the Quran. When I found that Islam didn't disregard Jesus, that was a big deal with me. Islam doesn't disregard any of the messengers and prophets – there's room for Adam, Noah, Jesus and finally the Prophet Muhammad.

Islam in Spanish founder Jaime Muhajid Fletcher was a Houston gang member before he converted and changed his ways.

> I didn't drink anymore. I didn't smoke anymore. I didn't go out. Not because someone told me to stop, but because I would have felt dirty if I'd done it. It was a total change. Deep inside, I wanted peace, and I wanted justice and for God to have given me Islam – it is what I hoped for all along.

Like many converts, Nahela Morales experienced rejection by her family at first, but the way she changed for the better, with good akhlaq, overcame this.

> Family members can feel betrayed until they see that this new path is only enhancing and bettering you. When I moved to New York, my parents worried that I would be clubbing and drinking. When I embraced Islam, it almost came as a relief to them. My grandmother in Mexico actually wears a scarf, covers her head, upon entering the church. The older generation does that. When I struck up a conversation about my hijab with her, it wasn't an alien concept.

Jalil Navarro too overcame initial rebuff, and conducted dawah by example. "They saw Islam in me and how it changed my life and the person I became. They said, 'Wow, this is amazing.'"

Similarly, Bianca Guerrero's family eventually came to accept her decision, too. In fact, both her mother and older sister converted to Islam. "Not my dad. He hasn't yet, but he's very proud of the woman I've become."

Some embraced the hip-hop culture of the 1990s when teenagers wore Malcolm X hats and read about the civil rights leader, including Alex Haley's *The Autobiography of Malcolm X*[4], also made into a 1992 film starring Denzel Washington. Parada elaborated: "I saw him going through that process and getting out of being a criminal." He also read how Malcolm X stopped hating white people after he traveled to Africa and the Middle East, and saw Muslims of all races worshiping together.

Finally, there has been a resurgence in Hispanics exploring their Andalusian roots, when Muslims governed Spain for 700 years until 1492.

1 Russ, V. (2019). More Latinos are becoming Muslims: "Islam is not as foreign as you think", *The Philadelphia Inquirer*, 5 May 2019. https://www.inquirer.com/news/latino-muslim-ramadan-philadelphia-converts-growing-islam-in-spanish-20190505.html

2 Turner, A. (2016). Spanish-language mosque in Houston draws worshippers. *The Huntsville Item*, 10 August 2016. https://www.itemonline.com/news/spanish-language-mosque-in-houston-draws-worshippers/article_ed6cf3fc-5f13-11e6-9a85-ebab01294a11.html

3 Claremont McKenna College (2017). *New report explores the identity of Latino Muslims in the United States*. https://www.cmc.edu/news/new-report-explores-identity-of-latino-muslims-in-united-states

Green, A. (2006). More US Hispanics drawn to Islam. *Christian Science Monitor*, 28 September 2006. https://www.csmonitor.com/2006/0928/p03s02-ussc.html

Martin, R. (2006). Latinas choosing Islam over Catholicism. *NPR*, 24 September 2006. https://web.archive.org/web/20210211012658/https://www.npr.org/templates/story/story.php?storyId=6133579

Mogahed, D. Kiramullah E. & Chouhoud, Y. (2022). American Muslim poll 2022: A POLITICS AND PANDEMIC STATUS REPORT. *Institute for Social Policy and Understanding*, 25 August 2022. https://www.ispu.org/american-muslim-poll-2022-1/

4 Malcolm X with Alex Haley (1965). *The autobiography of Malcolm X*. Grove Press. https://archive.org/details/the-autobiography-of-malcolm-x-as-told-to-alex-haley-malcolm-x-alex-haley-1992/0%20The%20autobiography%20of%20Malcolm%20X%2C%20as%20told%20to%20Alex%20Haley%20-%20Malcolm%20X%2C%20Alex%20Haley%20-%201992/mode/2up

43 Convert musicians

If you ask anyone, Muslim or non-Muslim, to name a Muslim convert musician, the first name that most people mention is Yusuf Islam. However, conversion to Islam has been popular for many years among musicians from different genres.

Most of the musicians below would be described as "cool." However, what many people miss is the fact that many musicians are also quite religious. It is not too fanciful to suggest that many of them are trying to capture the essence of reality (haqq) in their music, and that the process of writing music is one of inspiration.

Information about all the musicians below can be found on their pages in Wikipedia, and elsewhere on the internet.

Yusuf Islam

Yusuf Islam was born Steven Georgiou, to a Greek Cypriot father and Swedish mother, in London in 1948. In his youth, he excelled in music and art. At age 18, he secured a record deal and attained stardom, with a string of hits in the late 1960s and 1970s, under the stage name Cat Stevens. A girlfriend said his eyes were like those of a cat.

One experience that changed his outlook on life was contracting tuberculosis in 1969. This left him close to death, and he spent months in a hospital bed, during which time he contemplated his life and his attitude to religion. He investigated Buddhism, Zen, I Ching, numerology, tarot cards, astrology, meditation, yoga, and metaphysics.

Another near-death experience heightened his belief in God. While swimming off Malibu, he was caught in a rip tide that carried him out to sea. Nearly drowning, he shouted: "Oh, God! If you save me, I will work for you." Miraculously, a wave carried him back safely to shore.

Paradoxically his brother David converted to Judaism, but bought him a copy of the Quran on holiday, as he knew Steven's interest in world religions. While reading it, he was especially inspired by the story of Joseph, as contained in surah 12, converted to Islam, and took the name Yusuf Islam.

He founded Islamic schools in the UK, and established the Association of Muslim Schools (AMS-UK) in 1992. He has headed the Small Kindness and Muslim Aid charities.

He has won numerous awards for his humanitarian work, and for his music, as well as being conferred two honorary university doctorates.

A long-term tradition

Musicians have been converting to Islam for many decades. Many of them – and all the jazz musician converts listed below – are black, again emphasizing the color-blindness of Islam.

Joe Tex (1935 – 1982) (the stage name of Joseph Arrington Jr) was an American singer who mixed the styles of funk, country, gospel, and rhythm and blues. He converted in 1966, and changed his name to Yusuf Hazziez.

Danny Thompson (born 1939) is an English musician, playing the double bass and other instruments in folk-jazz, most famously with the group Pentangle. He converted in 1990.

Richard Thompson (born 1949) (no relation to Danny Thompson) is an English singer, songwriter, and guitarist, most famously with Fairport Convention. He converted in 1974.

Jermaine Jackson (born 1954) is most famous as an older brother of Michael Jackson, and a member of the Jackson Five. He has also had a solo career. He converted in 1989.

Indian converts

Kabir Suman (born Suman Chattopadhyay, 1949) is a music director, songwriter, singer, composer, politician, and former journalist. He converted from Hinduism in the 1990s in protest at the murder of an Australian Christian missionary by a Hindu fundamentalist group.

A. R. Rahman (an abbreviation of Allah Rakha Rahman, the name adopted on conversion by A. S. Dileep Kumar, born 1967) is an Indian film composer, record producer, singer and songwriter, predominantly in Tamil and Hindi films. He converted in his 20s. In 2009, he appeared in the *Time* list of the world's 100 most influential people.

Yuvan Shankar Raja (born 1979) is an Indian singer-songwriter and film score and soundtrack composer, mainly for Tamil films. He converted in 2014 and adopted the name Abdul Haliq.

Jazz

Two particular genres of music are well represented in Muslim converts. The first is jazz. A number of – especially American – jazz musicians converted in the middle of the last century.

Art (Arthur) Blakey (1919 – 1990) was an American jazz drummer and bandleader. He worked with famous jazz musicians including Thelonious Monk, Charlie Parker, and Dizzy Gillespie. He converted to Islam in the 1940s, and adopted the name Abdullah ibn Buhaina; however, he stopped being a practicing Muslim in the 1950s.

Yusef Abdul Lateef (born William Emanuel Huddleston, 1920 – 2013) was an American jazz multi-instrumentalist (saxophone, flute, oboe, bassoon, and other, Eastern instruments), and composer. He converted in the 1950s, and is credited as having played "world music" before the term existed.

Sahib Shihab (born Edmund Gregory, 1925 – 1989) was an American jazz saxophonist and flautist, who worked with Thelonious Monk, Dizzy Gillespie, John Coltrane and Quincy Jones. He was one of the first jazz musicians to convert to Islam, in 1947.

Vernel Fournier (1928 – 2000) was an American jazz drummer best known for his work with Ahmad Jamal from 1956 to 1962. He converted to Islam in 1975, and took the name Amir Rushdan.

Ahmad Jamal (born Frederick Russell Jones, 1930 - 2023) was an American jazz pianist, composer, bandleader and educator. He converted in 1950.

Abdullah Ibrahim (born 1934) is a South African pianist and composer. He was born Adolph Johannes Brand and before conversion went by the stage name Dollar Brand. During the apartheid era, he moved to Europe in 1962, and settled in New York City in 1965. He briefly returned to Cape Town in 1968, where he converted to Islam that year. He played with famous names, including the Duke Ellington Orchestra, and John Coltrane.

Idris Muhammad (born Leo Morris, 1939 – 2014) was an American jazz drummer with an extensive and varied career performing across jazz, funk, R'n'B and soul genres. He converted in the 1960s.

Rap and hip-hop

Similarly, a large number of modern rap and hip-hop artists have converted to Islam.

Akhenaton (born Philippe Fragione, 1968) is a French rapper and hip-hop producer of Italian origin.

Divine Styler (born Mark Richardson, 1968) is an American hip-hop artist. On conversion, he took the name Mikal Safiyullah.

Rakim (born William Michael Griffin Jr., 1968) is an American rapper and record producer. He converted in the 1980s.

MC Ren (born Lorenzo Jerald Patterson 1969) is an American rapper, songwriter and record producer. He converted in 1995.

Everlast (born Erik Francis Schrody, 1969) is an American musician, singer, rapper, and songwriter. He converted in 1996.

Ice Cube (born O'Shea Jackson Sr., 1969) is an American rapper, actor, and filmmaker. He converted in the 1990s.

Scarface (born Brad Terrence Jordan, 1970) is an American rapper and record producer. He converted in 2006.

*Q-Tip (*born Jonathan William Davis, 1970) is an American rapper, record producer, singer, actor and DJ. He converted in the mid-1990s, and took the name Kamaal ibn John Fareed.

Raekwon (born Corey Woods, 1970) is an American rapper and a member of Wu-Tang Clan. He converted in 2009.

Busta Rhymes (born Trevor George Smith Jr., 1972) is an American rapper. He converted in 2009.

Sean Price (stage name Ruckus, 1972 – 2015) was an American rapper. He converted in 2009.

Mos Def (born Dante Terrell Smith, 1973) is an American rapper, singer, songwriter, and actor. He converted to Islam in his teens and adopted the name Yasiin Bey.

Loon (born Chauncey Lamont Hawkins, 1975) is a former American rapper. He converted in 2008 and changed his name to Amir Junaid Muhadith.

Abd al Malik (born Régis Fayette-Mikano 1975) is a French rapper and spoken word artist of Congolese origin. He converted in 2002.

B.G. Knocc Out (born Arlandis Hinton, 1975) is an American West Coast rapper and songwriter. On conversion, he took the name Al Hasan Naqiyy.

One Be Lo (born Ralond Scruggs, 1976) is an American alternative hip hop artist. On conversion, he took the name Nahshid Sulaiman.

Vinnie Paz (born Vincenzo Luvineri, 1977) is a Sicilian American rapper.

The Jacka (born Dominick Newton, 1977 – 2015) was an American rapper. He converted at a young age and changed his name to Shaheed Akbar.

Others

Sinéad O'Connor (1966 – 2023) was an Irish-born singer, best known for her 1990 hit "Nothing Compares 2 U". She converted in 2018 and took the name Shuhada Davitt.

New Zealander *Jon Toogood* (born 1971) of the band Shihad converted in 2014.

Jennifer Grout (born 1990) is an American singer of Arabic and Amazigh music. She converted in 2013.

44 British career women converts

An article in the UK *Daily Mail* newspaper in 2010[1] described several prominent British career women who had converted to Islam.

A growing trend

This is a growing trend among modern British career women. Kevin Brice of Swansea University has studied the phenomenon.

> They seek spirituality, a higher meaning, and tend to be deep thinkers. The other type of women who turn to Islam are what I call 'converts of convenience.' They'll assume the trappings of the religion to please their Muslim husband and his family, but won't necessarily attend mosque, pray or fast.

Conversion to Islam is surprising, given the Islamophobia targeted at Muslims, in particular females. However, "Evidence suggests that the ratio of Western women converts to male could be as high as 2:1," says Brice. Female converts also seem more determined to display their faith – especially the hijab – in contrast to born-Muslims, who often go without the hijab. "Perhaps as a result of these actions, which tend to draw attention, white Muslims often report greater amounts of discrimination against them than do born Muslims."

An MTV presenter

Kristiane Backer is a German-born former MTV presenter now based in London. She had become disillusioned with the Western "anything goes" permissive society that turned out to be little more than a superficial void. In her book *From MTV to Mecca*[2], she recounted how she met and dated Imran Khan, the former cricketer, and former prime minister of Pakistan. She spent time with him in the Muslim country, where she was influenced by the spirituality and the warmth of the people.

> Though our relationship didn't last, I began to study the Muslim faith and eventually converted. Because of the nature of my job, I'd been out interviewing rock stars, travelling all over the world and

> following every trend, yet I'd felt empty inside. Now, at last, I had contentment because Islam had given me a purpose in life. In the West, we are stressed for superficial reasons, like what clothes to wear. In Islam, everyone looks to a higher goal. Everything is done to please God. It was a completely different value system. Despite my lifestyle, I realised how liberating it was to be a Muslim. To follow only one god makes life purer. You are not chasing every fad. I grew up in Germany in a not very religious Protestant family. I drank and I partied, but I realised that we need to behave well now so we have a good after-life. We are responsible for our own actions.

She encountered prejudice as soon as she converted.

> In Germany, there is Islamophobia. I lost my job when I converted. There was a Press campaign against me with insinuations about all Muslims supporting terrorists. I was vilified. Now, I am a presenter on NBC Europe. I call myself a European Muslim, which is different to the 'born' Muslim. I was married to one, a Moroccan, but it didn't work because he placed restrictions on me because of how he'd been brought up. As a European Muslim, I question everything. I don't accept blindly. But what I love is the hospitality and the warmth of the Muslim community. London is the best place in Europe for Muslims, there is wonderful Islamic culture here and I am very happy.

Indeed, London is nowadays a center for European Islam. According to the 2021 census, there are 1.3 million Muslims in London, 15% of the total population. There are estimated to be about 1,500 mosques in London. Open-air iftar and Eid events have taken place at various iconic venues, including Trafalgar Square and Wembley Stadium, largely thanks to the support of London's mayor, Sadiq Khan, a Muslim.

A DJ

Lynne Ali is from Dagenham in Essex, and describes herself as having been "a typical white hard-partying teenager".

> I would go out and get drunk with friends, wear tight and revealing clothing and date boys. I also worked part-time as a DJ, so I was

> really into the club scene. I used to pray a bit as a Christian, but I used God as a sort of doctor, to fix things in my life. If anyone asked, I would've said that, generally, I was happy living life in the fast lane.

Then she met and dated another student at university, Zahid, and a sea change in her attitude towards Islam and life in general took place.

> His sister started talking to me about Islam, and it was as if everything in my life fitted into place. I think, underneath it all, I must have been searching for something, and I wasn't feeling fulfilled by my hard-drinking party lifestyle.

Her conversion was abrupt, at age 19. "From that day, I started wearing the hijab and I now never show my hair in public. At home, I'll dress in normal Western clothes in front of my husband, but never out of the house."

A yoga teacher

The breakdown of traditional family values has led some women to convert. Brice comments: "Many people, from all walks of life, mourn the loss in today's society of traditional respect for the elderly and for women, for example. These are values which are enshrined in the Quran, which Muslims have to live by."

Camilla Leyland is a yoga teacher in Cornwall, and a single mother, who converted to Islam in her mid-20s for what she describes as "intellectual and feminist reasons".

> I know people will be surprised to hear the words "feminism" and "Islam" in the same breath, but in fact, the teachings of the Koran give equality to women, and at the time the religion was born, the teachings went against the grain of a misogynistic society. The big mistake people make is by confusing culture with religion. Yes, there are Muslim cultures which do not allow women individual freedom, yet when I was growing up, I felt more oppressed by Western society.

The change in her lifestyle became apparent to her when she:

went to an old friend's 21st birthday party in a bar. I walked in, wearing my hijab and modest clothing, and saw how everyone else had so much flesh on display. They were drunk, slurring their words and dancing provocatively. For the first time, I could see my former life with an outsider's eyes, and I knew I could never go back to that.

A former prime minister's sister-in-law

Perhaps the highest profile British female convert is Lauren Booth. She is the sister-in-law of Tony Blair, former British prime minister. She is also well-known in Britain as the daughter of actor Antony Booth from BBC TV's *Till Death Do Us Part*. She has written a book on her conversion[3].

It started when, as a journalist, she:

> … arrived alone in the West Bank to cover the elections there for *The Mail* on Sunday. It is safe to say that before that visit I had never spent any time with Arabs, or Muslims. So, as I flew towards the Middle East, my mind was full of the usual 10pm buzzwords: *radical extremists, fanatics, forced marriages, suicide bombers* and *jihad*.

However, when she came to meet everyday Muslims, she realized that this was a very distorted picture.

> My very first experience, though, could hardly have been more positive. I had arrived on the West Bank without a coat, as the Israeli airport authorities had kept my suitcase. Walking around the centre of Ramallah, I was shivering, whereupon an old lady grabbed my hand. Talking rapidly in Arabic, she took me into a house on a side street. Was I being kidnapped by a rather elderly terrorist? For several confusing minutes I watched her going through her daughter's wardrobe until she pulled out a coat, a hat and a scarf. I was then taken back to the street where I had been walking, given a kiss and sent warmly on my way. There had been not a single comprehensible word exchanged between us.

After she converted, she declared the news to her daughters. They made a list of questions they wanted answered.

> "Will you drink alcohol any more?" Answer: No. The response – a rather worrying "Yay!" "Will you smoke cigarettes any more?" Smoking isn't haram (forbidden) but it is harmful, so I answered: "No." Again, this was met with puritanical approval. Their final question, though, took me aback. "Will you have your breasts out in public now you are a Muslim?" What?? It seems they'd both been embarrassed by my plunging shirts and tops and had cringed on the school run at my pallid cleavage. Perhaps in hindsight I should have cringed as well. "Now that I'm Muslim," I said, "I will never have my breasts out in public again." "We love Islam!" they cheered and went off to play.

Kristiane Backer believes the new modern, independent Muslim women should unite to show the world from first-hand experience that Islam is not the repressive faith that it is often portrayed as.

> I know women – born Muslims – who became disillusioned and rebelled against it. When you dig deeper, it's not the faith they turned against, but the culture. Rules like marrying within the same sect or caste, and education being less important for girls, as they should get married anyway. Where does it say that in the Quran? It doesn't. Many young Muslims have abandoned the 'fire and brimstone' version they were born into, and have re-discovered a more spiritual and intellectual approach, that's free from the cultural dogmas of the older generation. That's how I intend to spend my life, showing the world the beauty of the true Islam.

1 Daily Mail (2010). Why ARE so many British career women converting to Islam? *The Daily Mail*, 28 October 2010. https://www.dailymail.co.uk/femail/article-1324039/Like-Lauren-Booth-ARE-modern-British-career-women-converting-Islam.html

2 Backer, K. (2012) *From MTV to Mecca: How Islam inspired my life*. Arcadia Books and Awakening Publications.

3 Booth, L. (2018) *Finding peace in the Holy Land: A British Muslim memoir*. Kube Publishing.

45 Tauhid and Christianity

One of the major themes of this book, because it is one of the most central beliefs of Islam, is that there is one, and only one, God. The Arabic word for this is *tauhid*, related to the word *ahad* meaning "one" (see Chapter 23).

The two religions with the largest number of followers today are Christianity and Islam (see Chapter 46). Tauhid is one of the main reasons that people convert from Christianity to Islam. Sinéad O'Connor (see Chapter 43) has said what many converts to Islam say, namely that she grew up in an (at least nominally) Christian environment, and believed in a higher being (God), but could not understand the position that is given to Jesus (Isa) in Christianity. "The Christ character tells us himself: you must only talk directly to the Father; you don't need intermediaries."[1]

Jesus believed in tauhid

The teachings of Jesus (Isa) correspond to Muslim belief in many ways. Muslims see no contradiction in this, as Jesus is considered the second-to-last prophet of God (Muhammad, pbuh, being the last). One of these beliefs is that Jesus believed in one God, as recorded in the Bible (Mark 12:28-34):

> And one of the scribes came, and having heard them reasoning together, and perceiving that he had answered them well, asked him: "Which is the first commandment of all?" And Jesus answered him: "The first of all the commandments *is*, Hear, O Israel; The Lord our God is one Lord: And thou shalt love the Lord thy God with all thy heart, and with all thy soul, and with all thy mind, and with all thy strength." … And the scribe said unto him: "Well, Master, thou hast said the truth: for there is one God; and there is none other but he: And to love him with all the heart, and with all the understanding, and with all the soul, and with all the strength … is more than all whole burnt offerings and sacrifices." And when Jesus saw that he answered discreetly, he said unto him: "Thou art not far from the kingdom of God."

Several things are worth noting from this.

Firstly, Muslims will recognize Jesus's saying "Hear, O Israel; The Lord our God is one Lord" as being very similar to Surat al-Ikhlas (112): "Say, 'He is God, the One. God, the Absolute. He begets not, nor was He begotten. And there is none comparable to Him.'"

Secondly, it is important to note that Jesus said that there is only one God, but he did not say that he himself was God in any way. In other words, it is important to note not only what Jesus said, but also what he did not say.

There is a spectrum of views within Christianity about the divinity of Jesus. Most modern Christians believe that Jesus was in some literal sense the son of God, that is, at least partly divine. In Islam, this is a form of *shirk*, that is, associating someone or something with God, thereby implying that others are on a par with God. In the Quran (4:48), God Himself states that this is the one thing He will not forgive: "God does not forgive association with Him, but He forgives anything less than that to whomever He wills. Whoever associates anything with God has devised a monstrous sin."

Thirdly, Jesus said: "The Lord our God is one Lord." Note the word *our*. So, Jesus is saying that the Lord is my (Jesus's) God and your God. Jesus is acknowledging God as his (Jesus's) God.

Unitarian belief in tauhid

It was written above that "*most* modern Christians believe that Jesus was in some literal sense the son of God". It may surprise readers to learn that there are some Christians who do not believe this. That is, they do believe in one God, and that Jesus was not God in any sense. One such group are known as Unitarians (*uni-* meaning "one"), in contrast to most Christians, who are Trinitarians (*tri-* meaning "three").

Trinitarians define God as three persons: God the Father, God the Son (i.e. Jesus), and God the Holy Spirit (referred to more often as the Holy Ghost in the King James Bible). However, they are all considered divine. Unitarians, on the other hand, understand God as one entity. They thus adhere to strict monotheism and they maintain that Jesus was a great man and a great prophet of God, but not God himself. This, of course, corresponds to the Muslim view of one God (tauhid), and of Jesus being a great prophet, but without doubt wholly a human being.

In places in the Bible, Jesus is referred to as a prophet.

"And when he was come into Jerusalem, all the city was moved, saying: 'Who is this?' And the multitude said: 'This is Jesus the prophet of Nazareth of Galilee'" (Matthew 21:10-11).

"The woman saith unto him [Jesus], 'Sir, I perceive that thou art a prophet'" (John 4:19).

History of Unitarianism

Unitarianism started, seemingly independently, in Poland-Lithuania, Transylvania (central Romania), England and the USA. The first Unitarian Church in England was established in 1774 in Essex Street, London, the site of the current British Unitarian headquarters. In the USA, King's Chapel in Boston officially adopted Unitarian doctrine in 1784. Its rector, James Freeman, revised the Prayer Book according to Unitarian doctrines in 1786.

Famous Unitarians, past and present, include Louisa May Alcott (US novelist and poet), Béla Bartók (Hungarian composer), Tim Berners-Lee (English inventor of the World Wide Web), Charles Darwin (English naturalist), Charles Dickens (English writer), Ralph Waldo Emerson (US essayist), Paul Newman (US actor), Kurt Vonnegut (US writer), Frank Lloyd Wright (US architect and designer), as well as five presidents of the USA: John Adams, John Quincy Adams, Millard Fillmore, Thomas Jefferson, and William Howard Taft.

Unitarian beliefs

There is no definitive, authoritative statement of the beliefs of Unitarianism. However, Unitarians generally believe in the following:

- The oneness of God
- The life and teachings of Jesus as an example for humans to follow. While Unitarians, being essentially Christians, do not accept the prophethood of Muhammad, the parallel is clear here between Unitarian Christians regarding the life and teachings of Jesus as a model to be followed, and Muslims

regarding the life and teachings (hadiths) of Muhammad as a model to be followed.

- Faith is compatible with reason, science and philosophy. Note Charles Darwin's name above among the list of famous Unitarians. Other famous Unitarian scientists and inventors include Erasmus Darwin (physician, grandfather of Charles Darwin), Joseph Priestley (English chemist), Sir Isaac Newton (English scientist in many fields), and George Boole (English mathematician).
- Free will
- Rejection of the Christian concept of original sin. This is the doctrine that, because of the sin of Adam by disobedience to God in the Garden of Eden, mankind (the descendants of Adam and Eve, Hawwa) is in a state of sin. This original sin can only be atoned by belief in Christianity and its view of Jesus.
- Rejection of the Atonement, that is, the forgiving or pardoning of sin through the death of Jesus by crucifixion
- The human authorship of the Bible in use today. This differs from the original message (Injil) give to Jesus. Today's version is therefore subject to human error.

Christian Science belief in tauhid

Another group rejecting the divine nature of Jesus is Christian Science (or the Church of Christ, Scientist, to give it its official name), which was founded by Mary Baker Eddy in the USA in the late 19th century CE. In the early 20th, it was the fastest growing religion in the USA, with 270,000 members in 1936, but that figure has now shrunk to around 50,000. Because of its shrinking numbers, the church's *Christian Science Monitor*, first published in 1908, was eventually printed weekly rather than daily, and now only publishes an online version.

Like Unitarianism, Christian Science rejects, or at least provides very different interpretations of, core Christian concepts including the trinity, the divinity of Jesus, his crucifixion and atonement, and his resurrection.

Famous people who are or were Christian Scientists include Richard Bach (US author), Joan Crawford (US actor), Doris Day (US actor, singer), Kelsey Grammer (US actor), Joyce Grenfell (UK comedian), Val Kilmer (US actor), Mike Nesmith (US musician), Sergei Prokofiev (Russian composer), Ginger Rogers (US actor, dancer, singer), J. D. Salinger (US author), Alan Shepard (US astronaut), and Danielle Steele (US author).

There seem to be many similarities between Unitarian Christianity, Christian Science, and Islam. They mostly stem from the belief in one, and only one, God (tauhid), and therefore the status of Jesus as a human prophet of God.

In the Quran (5:82), God says: "You will find that the nearest in affection towards the believers are those who say: 'We are Christians.'" It seems that the Christians that are closest to Muslims are the Unitarians and the Christian Scientists, as their beliefs about Christianity, Jesus and the Bible are very similar to those of Muslims.

This is not to say that Unitarians and Christian Scientists are Muslims. They may agree with the first half of the declaration of faith, that there is only one God worthy of worship. However, they do not believe in the second half, namely that Muhammad is the prophet of God, with the concomitant belief that the Quran, that was revealed to Muhammad, is the word of God.

1 Channel 4 News (2013). *Jon Snow interview with Sinéad O'Connor*. https://www.youtube.com/watch?v=SB9F6YoyxJA

46 Born Muslims, Muslim converts, and culture

World Muslim population

How many Muslims are there in the world? It is difficult to give a precise answer, as figures for some counties are hard to come by. Figures reported by various bodies are thus at best estimates. Figures taken from censuses may be deceptive, as they always rely on self-reporting, that is, someone ticking a box about themselves. Someone may tick "Muslim," but nobody checks by knocking on their door and asking them to list the five pillars, recite a couple of surahs, admit whether they did the five daily prayers the day before, or fasted during Ramadan.

The Pew Research Center describes itself as "a nonpartisan fact tank that informs the public about the issues, attitudes and trends shaping the world. We conduct public opinion polling, demographic research, content analysis and other data-driven social science research."[1] A major area of its research is "religion and public life."[2]

In 2015, Pew published the results of a survey[3] entitled *The future of world religions: Population growth projections, 2010-2050. Why Muslims are rising fastest and the unaffiliated are shrinking as a share of the world's population*. This was followed in 2017 by further reports[4,5] attempting to account for these changes.

Logically, there are three possible reasons why the figures for religious populations might change: (i) fertility (the number of babies born to women), (ii) conversions to the religion, and (iii) conversions from the religion (apostasy). Pew's 2017 reports point out that the rise in the Muslim population is mostly due to the first of these.

What is the population of the world? It has risen alarmingly in the last century. In 1900, there were 1.65 billion people in the world. This rose to 2.53 b in 1950, 3.02 b in 1960, 3.68 b in 1970, 4.44 b in 1980, 5.31 b in 1990, 6.13 b in 2000, 6.93 b in 2010, and 7.84 b in 2020. The figure at the time of writing (2023) is 8.05 b.

What are the causes of this skyrocketing population? Ranga[6] gives 11:

1. Better healthcare, e.g. eradication of diseases, and people living longer

2. Rise in birthrate, e.g. fewer deaths of mothers and babies during childbirth

3. Food security, e.g. greater availability of food in most parts of the world

4. Lack of awareness/education, e.g. women with low education tend to have more children

5. Cultural influences, e.g. attitudes towards age of marriage, societal pressure

6. Lack of family planning, e.g. knowledge of, and use of, contraception

7. Religious propagation, e.g. encouragement from preachers, increasing the population of their religion

8. Malicious intent to change demographics, e.g. "ethnic cleansing"

9. Immigration, e.g. biased migration policies to raise particular vote banks

10. For social support, e.g. in agricultural societies, children becoming workers

11. Perception of marriage and family, e.g. attitudes towards marriage and children

Pew[4] predict that babies born to Muslims will outnumber those born to Christians (by far the two largest religious groups worldwide) by 2035. Between 2015 and 2060, the overall world population will rise by 32%, but Muslims are the only religious group above this average, at 70%. Pew[5] conclude: "In the next half century or so [i.e. before the end of this century], Christianity's long reign as the world's largest religion may come to an end." They attribute this to the birth rate, which leads to the Muslim population having a lower average age, and more young people getting married and having children.

Most commentators point out that the numbers of conversions to Islam, and conversions from Islam, are small compared with the birth rate.

British Muslim convert population

A 2011 article[7] by Sarfraz Manzoor, a British Muslim of Pakistani heritage, comments on the rate of conversion in the UK: "A report this week suggested the number of converts had doubled in the past 10 years from about 60,000 in 2001 to up to 100,000 with around 5,200 people converting to Islam in the UK last year." This is surprising, given the attacks in that period by people claiming to be Muslims: among others, the 9/11 attacks in the USA, and in the UK, the 7/7 bombings, the murder of British soldier Lee Rigby, and the Westminster and London Bridge attacks.

Reasons for conversion

As we have seen in previous chapters, Islam is a religion of peace, and these attacks were all condemned immediately by religious authorities[8]. As Sarfraz Manzoor asks: "Why are people voluntarily signing up to a faith that is, if you believe what you read, a cesspit of misogyny, violence and hate?"

One reason offered is that the 9/11 attacks brought Islam into the media. "Following the attacks there was an understandable rise in focus on the faith, which led non-Muslims to want to find out more about the religion that was now so often in the news."

Another reason for the rise in the number of Muslims in the UK, that is, people ticking the "Muslim" box in a census, is the fact that mixed-faith marriages (born Muslims marrying born non-Muslims) are now common. Sarfraz Manzoor calls these "conversions of convenience", and it seems that this happened to him too. "When I got married my family asked my fiancée to convert but she was rightly reluctant and I had always been uneasy about the cynicism of such conversions and felt it demeaned those people who had truly changed faith." He was also wary of the number of female converts wearing hijab. "It was as if these women needed to advertise their newfound faith in a way that my sister, mother and sister-in-law – none of them hijab wearers – did not need to."

As reported in previous chapters, he notes that the majority of converts in the UK are female, and that conversions are driven by dissatisfaction with the Western way of life, with the normalization of immoral behavior – alcohol and drunkenness, a lack of morality and sexual permissiveness, and unrestrained consumerism – among an increasingly irreligious British public. He finds this ironic when compared to born Muslims in the UK. "At a time when British Muslims of Asian extraction are increasingly drinking and engaging in sexual permissiveness, white converts are fleeing towards piety."

Islam and culture

Sarfraz Manzoor admits to being jealous of British Muslim converts, as they have certain advantages over born Muslims, mostly to do with the lack of cultural baggage. British Muslim converts have not grown up in a Muslim environment, and have thus seen Islam from both sides: as a non-Muslim, and as a convert Muslim. Having grown up in the UK – a Christian and some would say post-Christian environment – they are better positioned to evaluate the similarities and differences between Islam and Christianity. Converts have decided to investigate Islam, and often done substantial reading on the subject, before coming to the crunch question "Should I convert?" with its concomitant issues, frequently being, rejection by family. As a result, Sarfraz Manzoor submits that "they know far more about Islam than most British Pakistanis."

Even if they were born and brought up in the UK, British Pakistanis still have Pakistani parents and families, and "the conservatism of our working-class Pakistani culture blurred into the way our families practised religion." That is, it was often difficult to distinguish Islamic culture (as contained in the textual authority of the Quran and Sunnah) and Pakistani culture (as practiced in Pakistan, and now in the UK, but often taken to be the same as Islamic culture). Sarfraz Manzoor suggests that converts:

> … are not weighed down by the same baggage and thus can be a useful bridge between cultures and in nudging other Muslims towards a more liberal and tolerant direction on issues such as mixing between men and women in mosques and mixed-faith marriages.

Sarfraz Manzoor ends with a paradox:

> It used to be said that Asians – with their emphasis on family values, hard work and education – were "more British than the British". It is a final irony that today it could be argued that converts to Islam, with their ability to disentangle faith from culture, are now more Muslim than their brown brothers and sisters in faith.

1 Pew Research Center (n.d.). https://www.pewresearch.org

2 Wikipedia (n.d.). *Pew Research Center*. https://en.wikipedia.org/wiki/Pew_Research_Center

3 Pew Research Center (2015). The future of world religions: Population growth projections, 2010-2050. Why Muslims are rising fastest and the unaffiliated are shrinking as a share of the world's population. *Pew Research Center*, 2 April 2015. https://www.pewresearch.org/religion/2015/04/02/religious-projections-2010-2050/

4 Pew Research Center (2017). The changing global religious landscape. *Pew Research Center*, 5 April 2017. https://www.pewresearch.org/religion/2017/04/05/the-changing-global-religious-landscape

5 Pew Research Center (2017). Why Muslims are the world's fastest-growing religious group. *Pew Research Center*, 6 April 2017. https://www.pewresearch.org/fact-tank/2017/04/06/why-muslims-are-the-worlds-fastest-growing-religious-group

6 Ranga, N. R. (2022). 10 causes of population growth: Possible implications. *Mind Controversy.* https://www.mindcontroversy.com/causes-of-population-growth/#:~:text=10%20Causes%20of%20Population%20Growth%20%7C%20Possible%20Implications,to%20manipulate%20democracy%20by%20demography%20...%20More%20items

7 Sarfraz Manzoor (2011). What we Muslims can learn from converts. *The Guardian*, 6 January 2011. https://www.theguardian.com/commentisfree/belief/2011/jan/06/muslim-islam-uk-pakistan

8 Kurzmann, C. (2020). *Islamic statements against terrorism*. University of North Carolina. https://kurzman.unc.edu/islamic-statements-against-terrorism

Brief Glossary of Arabic Islamic Terms

Adab: Islamic etiquette
Akhlaq: The Islamic practice of virtue, morality, good manners and character
Allah: God in Arabic
Ansar: (literally "helpers") Residents of Madinah who became Companions
Asma ul-husna: The 99 names of Allah, epithets (nouns or adjectives; words or phrases) describing His attributes
Asr: Afternoon prayer
Athan: The call to prayer
Aurah: Private parts that should be covered: male and female genitals, and for adult females the breasts
Ayah: Verse of the Quran (literally "sign")
Dai: Someone who performs dawah
Dawah: Invitation to Islam
Dua: Supplication (see Chapter 2)
Fajr: Dawn prayer
Fard: Obligatory
Fitrah: The innate human state, with a disposition to acknowledge one God.
Hadith: Reported teaching of Prophet Muhammad
Hadith qudsi: A hadith where Muhammad is quoting Allah
Hafith: Someone, male or female, who has memorized the whole Quran
Hajj: Pilgrimage to Makkah (a pillar of Islam)
Halal: Permissible, applicable to all everyday activities, especially food
Haram: Forbidden, applicable to all everyday activities
Iftar: Breaking of fast at Maghrib time
Ihsan: Consciousness of the omnipresence of Allah (see Chapter 4)
Imam: Prayer leader
Iman: Faith
Isha: Dusk prayer
Islam: Surrender to Allah (see Chapter 25)
Isra Miraj: The miraculous night journey when Muhammad went from Makkah to Jerusalem, and then ascended to the heavens

Jahannam: Hell
Jannah: Paradise
Jinn: An invisible being
Kabah: The black cube-shaped building which is the focus and direction of Muslim prayer
Khushu: Humility and concentration in prayer
Kufr: Disbelief
Maghrib: Sunset prayer
Makruh: Discouraged actions
Masjid: Mosque
Masjid al-Haram: The mosque in Makkah containing the Kabah
Mathhab: Islamic school of thought
Muathin: Person who makes the call to prayer (athan)
Mubah: Neutral actions that carry neither rewards nor penalties
Mustahab: Encouraged actions
Nafs: Base desires (literally "self")
Niat: Intention
Qiblah: Direction of prayer towards Makkah
Quran: The holy book of Islam (literally "recitation')
Rabb: Lord, master (literally "sustainer, cherisher")
Rakaah: Cycle of prayer
Ruku: Bending during salah prayer
Ramadan: The ninth month of the Islamic lunar calendar, during which Muslims fast
Sabr: Patience
Sadaqah: Charity (see Chapter 10)
Sadaqah jariyah: Charity with long-term benefits
Sahur: Meal before starting each day's fast at Fajr prayer time in Ramadan
Salah: Prayer (see Chapter 2) (the five daily prayers, a pillar of Islam)
Shahadah: Declaration of faith; also, the definition of a Muslim (a pillar of Islam)
Shaitan: Satan, the Devil
Sawm: Fasting (during Ramadan, a pillar of Islam)
Sujud: Prostration during salah prayer
Sunnah: The practice of Muhammad, as contained in the hadiths
Surah: Chapter of the Quran

Tafsir: Commentary on the Quran
Tajwid: Rules of reciting the Quran
Taqwa: God-consciousness
Thikr: Remembrance of Allah
Thuhr: Midday prayer
Ummah: A community, often used for the worldwide Muslim community
Umrah: Pilgrimage to Makkah outside the Hajj period
Wajib: Obligatory
Wudu: Washing before salah prayers
Zakah: Compulsory charity (a pillar of Islam)